Australian Wildlife

A VISITOR'S GUIDE

Stella Martin

www.bradtguides.com

Bradt Travel Guides Ltd, UK
The Globe Pequot Press Inc, USA

edition

Reprinted September 2013
First published July 2010

Bradt Travel Guides Ltd
IDC House, The Vale, Chalfont St Peter, Bucks SL9 9RZ, England
www.bradtguides.com
Print edition published in the USA by The Globe Pequot Press Inc,
PO Box 480, Guilford, Connecticut 06437-0480

ISBN: 978 1 84162 324 5 (print)

British Library Cataloguing in Publication Data
A catalogue record for this book is available from the British Library

Photographs
Stella Martin (SM); Ian Montgomery (IM); Steven Nowakowski (SN); Kerry Trapnell (KT);
Denis Walls (DW); Greg Watson (GW); Daniel Webster (DJW); Wrights Air

The following photographs are supplied courtesy of Frank Lane Picture Library:
Theo Allofs/Minden Pictures (TA/FLPA); Christo Baars/FN/Minden Pictures (CB/FLPA);
Fred Bavendam/Minden Pictures (FB/FLPA); Neil Bowman (NB/FLPA); Claver Carroll
(CC/FLPA); Reinhard Dirscherl (RD/FLPA); Gerry Ellis/Minden Pictures (GE/FLPA); Michael
and Patricia Fogden/Minden Pictures (M&PF/FLPA); Andrew Forsyth (AF/FLPA); Foto Natura
Stock (FNS/FLPA); Tom and Pam Gardner (T&PG/FLPA); Bob Gibbons (BG/FLPA); Christian
Handl/Imagebroker (CH/FLPA); David Hosking (DH/FLPA); Mitsuhiko Imamori/Minden
Pictures (MI/FLPA); Mitsuaki Iwago/Minden Pictures (MIW/FLPA); Gerard Lacz (GL/FLPA);
Frans Lanting (FL/FLPA); Scott Linstead/Minden Pictures (SL/FLPA); Thomas Marent/Minden
Pictures (TM/FLPA); Chris Mattison (CM/FLPA); Alan Parker (AP/FLPA); Mike Parry/Minden
Pictures (MP/FLPA); Cyril Ruoso/Minden Pictures (CR/FLPA); Jurgen and Christine Sohns
(J&CS/FLPA); Krystyna Szulecka (KS/FLPA); Martin B Withers (MW/FLPA); Eric Woods
(EW/FLPA); Konrad Wothe/Minden Pictures (KW/FLPA); Shin Yoshino/Minden Pictures
(SY/FLPA); Gerhard Zwerger-SC (GZ/FLPA); ZSSD/Minden Pictures (ZD/FLPA)

Front cover, main image: koala (ZD/FLPA)
Front cover, inset images (from left to right): crimson rosella (J&CS/FLPA);
thorny devil (MIW/FLPA); red-eyed treefrog (MW/FLPA)
Back cover: buff-breasted paradise-kingfisher (IM)
Title page (from top to bottom):
red kangaroo (FL/FLPA); rainbow lorikeet (IM); harlequin tuskfish (GW)

Maps
Malcolm Barnes

Designed and formatted by Chris Lane, Artinfusion (www.artinfusion.co.uk)
Production managed by Jellyfish Print Solutions; printed in India

CONTENTS

AUTHOR AND PHOTOGRAPHERS

Stella Martin grew up in Northern Ireland, fascinated by the natural world and determined to travel. Teaching English in various parts of the world, she spent her spare time investigating, and writing about, the local environment. In 1990 she moved to Australia and was employed by Queensland Parks and Wildlife Service to write the very popular *Tropical Topics*, an educational newsletter on the wildlife of north Queensland. This work was recognised by the Wet Tropics Management Authority in 2008, when she was presented with a Cassowary Award. She has written numerous freelance articles on travel and wildlife and in 2006 won second prize in the *BBC Wildlife* magazine travel writing competition. www.stellabridgetmartin.com

Ian Montgomery (IM) became a keen birdwatcher as a schoolboy in Ireland in the 1960s. Having graduated in zoology, he moved to Australia in 1971 and became seriously interested in bird photography in 1988. His impressive collection, used extensively by Birds Australia, can be seen at: www.birdway.com.au

Steven Nowakowski (SN) is a renowned landscape photographer who runs his own publishing business, producing cards, posters, books and calendars. He recently opened his Photographic Wilderness Gallery in Cairns to showcase his images. www.stevennowakowski.com

Greg Watson (GW), a professional zookeeper, has spent his life working with wildlife, including a stint as a venomous snake collector (for venom extraction). He is a champion of small, underappreciated animals, such as invertebrates and Australian freshwater fishes, but snakes are never far from his heart.

Kerry Trapnell (KT) specialises in capturing images of the landscapes and Aboriginal people of Cape York Peninsula. He is an internationally recognised photographer whose work has been commissioned by *National Geographic* and the World Wide Fund for Nature. He has also worked for many Australian agencies and NGOs.

Daniel Webster (DJW) is a PADI scuba instructor and underwater photographer. www.underwatersnap.com

ACKNOWLEDGEMENTS

I would first like to thank Hilary Bradt for inviting me to write this book and Mike Unwin for his close attention, wise edits, awkward questions and patient emails. Also designer Chris Lane, at Artinfusion, and Anna Moores and other friendly members of the Bradt team. Here in Australia, I would particularly like to thank my husband, Denis Walls, for his role as companion, driver, photographer, editor, advisor and meal provider. I am very grateful to Rupert Russell, who very kindly read and commented on much of the text, as well as to Greg Watson and Terry Vallance for checking sections. Many more patiently answered my bothersome queries and, over the years, countless people have generously shared their knowledge with me. On our various research trips many friends, old and new, welcomed us into their homes. I would like to thank families Guy, Cullen, Rotherham, Neilsen and Mau, Val Schier, John Boulton, Lindy Marlowe and Cameron Walls. I would also like to acknowledge the generous assistance of Tourism NT. Finally, I'd like to acknowledge the birds, skinks, spiders, flying-foxes, tadpoles, butterflies and bandicoot outside my window that both diverted me and kept me on track.
Dedicated to Denis, Liam and Cameron.

INTRODUCTION

Australia is huge: the sixth largest country in the world and the only one to occupy an entire continental landmass. With a total area of approximately 7,692,030 km², it is nearly 32 times the size of the United Kingdom and roughly equal to the 48 contiguous states of the United States. This immense landscape dwarfs its population of only 21.5 million and, rare in today's world, there are vast tracts of wilderness with no sign of human intervention.

Australia is also a land of spectacular contrasts. Spanning more than 30 degrees of latitude from north to south, 42% of its land mass lies within the tropics yet its southern coasts are whipped by Antarctic gales. This ancient landscape is celebrated as 'the wide, brown land' but in addition to the iconic, ochre rockscapes of the arid outback there are great expanses of forest, rugged mountains, alpine heathlands, tropical wetlands, empty beaches lapped by clear, turquoise seas and the largest coral reef on the planet. It is possible to watch mobs of kangaroos bounding across the plains, koalas slouching on branches, platypuses diving in pristine creeks, birds of paradise displaying in rainforest treetops, crocodiles sunning themselves on tropical riverbanks and wombats snuffling through the snow. Thanks to the continent's lengthy isolation from other land masses, much of its flora and fauna is endemic: about 85% of flowering plants, 84% of mammals, over 45% of birds and nearly 90% of inshore temperate-zone fishes are found nowhere else in the world. Australia, in short, is a very special place for wildlife.

As the heat of the day fades, kangaroos bound off for a night's grazing. (MIW/FLPA)

ABOUT THIS BOOK

This book is not a field guide but a portable, compact overview of the most interesting aspects of Australia's wildlife, and where best to observe it. A number of excellent field guides are available to assist with identification but this book, while introducing some of the more common animals, also places them in a meaningful context and offers insights into their often curious behaviour.

Initial chapters set the scene. *The Backdrop* (page 3) explains how the landscape developed over aeons and how the wildlife evolved in response to a changing environment. It also takes into account the human impact, including current conservation issues, and prevailing climatic conditions. *Habitats* (page 19) looks at the various ecosystems, with a focus on significant components of the vegetation communities, and indicates briefly how different conditions have produced behavioural traits in animals. The core of the book consists of five chapters dedicated to principal taxonomic groups: *Mammals, Birds, Reptiles, Amphibians and Freshwater Fishes* and *Invertebrates*. They do not attempt to list all species – impossible in a book of this size – but provide interesting background information with a focus on some frequently encountered creatures. Another chapter, *The Marine Environment* (page 143), takes an underwater view of both tropical seas (including the Great Barrier Reef) and lesser-known temperate waters. *Where to Go* (page 157) provides a state-by-state summary of basic geography and key destinations for wildlife spotting. *Top Tips* (page 179) provides practical advice for the visitor and *Further Reading* (page 188) recommends a variety of field guides and other books for background information.

A male orange-thighed tree frog (*Litoria xanthomera*) calls for a mate. (GW)

THE BACKDROP

A fig tree root seeks out water on the rust-red cliffs of Queensland's Lawn Hill Gorge. (GW)

THE LAND, PAST AND PRESENT

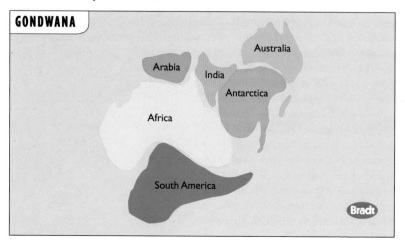

Gondwana, 150 million years ago.

PAST UPHEAVALS

Like any other land mass, Australia has had its ups and downs. Once there were mountains comparable in size to today's Himalayas and Andes, but the aeons have seen more erosion than construction and it now ranks as the lowest and flattest of all continents. However, it is by no means featureless.

Australia, along with South America, Africa, India and Antarctica, was once part of the great supercontinent, Gondwana. About 150 million years ago this huge land mass began to break up, South America, Africa and India sliding off in their own directions, leaving Australia connected to Antarctica. The world was warmer then so, in spite of its southerly position, life flourished. A shallow inland sea covered much of Australia about this time; fossilised marine creatures and petrified ripples imprinted in sandstone rocks are found in today's bone-dry interior.

About 50 million years ago, Australia made the final split from Antarctica and started moving north, a journey that continues today at about 6–10cm a year – the rate at which a human hair grows. (At this speed it should straddle the Equator in about 40 million years.) Along the way the continent has been passing over a volcanic hotspot, which currently lies dormant between Tasmania and the mainland. Periodically this has forced lava to the surface, creating a line of volcanoes along the east coast. Most notable of these is the 22-million-year-old Tweed Volcano on the Queensland–New South Wales border, now reduced to a massive caldera.

About 15 million years ago Australia rammed the southeast Asian plate, the crumple zone between the two land masses rising up to create the highlands of what is now New Guinea. As the world entered a cooler, drier phase, sea levels fell (because water was captured in polar ice caps), creating land bridges from mainland Australia to southeast Asia and Tasmania.

THE LANDSCAPE TODAY

Australia's most significant landform today is the Great Dividing Range, a series of mountains, hills and plateaus with an escarpment edge facing generally east, that runs parallel to the east coast for 3,500km from Cape York Peninsula, in north Queensland, to the southeast corner where its highest section is known as the Australian Alps. It then takes a westward turn through Victoria – and resurfaces in Tasmania. Many of the older sedimentary and metamorphic rocks have been

Rocks of the arid interior preserve ripples from an ancient inland sea. (SM)

eroded away, leaving granite intrusions as the higher peaks. Although greater in length than in height – its average elevation is below 1,000m, and its highest point (Mount Kosciuszko) is just 2,228m – this range profoundly affects the entire continent by causing most rain to fall on the eastern seaboard and creating a rain shadow over the interior.

To the west of the Great Dividing Range the land slopes gently away and becomes increasingly arid. Vast, flat, dry plains are braided with habitually dry river channels and punctuated with sandstone and limestone escarpments. These rocky outcrops – products of sedimentation, tilting and folding from hundreds of millions of years ago – create some of Australia's most distinctive scenery. Often harbouring permanent water, they provide oases for plants and animals in an otherwise harsh environment. Although the underlying rock is usually white or grey in colour, throughout central Australia cliffs and sand grains alike glow rust-red thanks to layers of iron oxide cemented to the surface by microscopic fungi.

Kata Tjuta is the visible tip of a deep sandstone slab. (SM)

Below the arid surface, huge quantities of water lie out of sight in artesian basins, which underlie 60% of the continent – and make modern human occupation of the arid centre possible. The largest, the Great Artesian Basin, extends for over 1.7 million km^2 below Queensland, South Australia, New South Wales and the Northern Territory, and contains an estimated 64,900 million megalitres of water (equal to 32,450 million Olympic swimming pools), some of it almost two million years old. It is topped up as rainfall seeps in along the eastern edge of the Great Dividing Range and travels through the porous rock.

Two massive river basins occupy nearly one-third of the continent. Waters in the largest, the Lake Eyre drainage system, never reach the sea, terminating instead in Australia's largest lake. Just don't expect to go swimming there. For most of the time Lake Eyre is a vast, dry, salt pan which fills with water only a few times each century. Most of the water originates in Queensland. Poor flows peter out in the branching alluvial fans of the Channel Country but stronger flows, after months of travelling, may reach the lake. When this happens it explodes with life as waterbirds converge to breed.

Next door (in continental terms), to the southwest, the massive one-million-km^2 basin of the Murray and Darling rivers drains water from inland Queensland, New South Wales and Victoria to the Murray's mouth near Adelaide. Much of this water is diverted for agriculture; this is the nation's food basket, producing three-quarters of the country's irrigated crops and pastures, and one-third of its agricultural output – but not without an environmental cost (see *Water pressures*, page 13).

A rare sight: water in Lake Eyre, April 2009. (Wrights Air)

In recent geological times the continent has been very static, with erosion outweighing construction. Soil-creating processes have been minimal – there has been little uplifting, almost no glaciation and limited volcanic action – but, over millions of years, the relentless weathering of existing soils has leached them of nutrients. These infertile soils are fundamental to a chain reaction that ripples right through the natural world. Plants growing on them are tough, often filled with toxins and low in nutrition.

Erosion has reduced Australia's highest point, Mount Kosciuszko, to 2,228m. (SM)

They provide poor food for herbivores and, consequently, for the animals that prey on them. Combined with the harsh, unpredictable climate, these poor soils have been a major driving force behind the evolution of Australia's flora and fauna.

EVOLUTION – MOVING WITH THE TIMES

Australia's plants and animals have their roots in the Gondwanan past. A band of broadleaf rainforest once stretched from present-day South America, through Antarctica, to Australia, and animals migrated back and forth as they evolved. Gondwanan echoes exist today in Australia: Tasmanian forests are similar to the *Nothofagus* forests of Chile; a Queensland stag beetle (*Sphaenognathus queenslandiae*) must look to the Andes to find its closest relative; fossilised teeth from an early form of platypus (when they had teeth) have turned up in southern Argentina.

The first marsupials evolved at about this time. They were once thought to be primitive forerunners of placental animals but it is now known that marsupials are a distinct branch of the mammalian evolutionary tree. Despite their modern distribution, they actually evolved in the northern hemisphere – the earliest known marsupial fossil, dating back 125 million years, was found in China – and it is believed they spread through North and South America (where some still survive) and across Antarctica, reaching Australia before the final break-up of Gondwana. It had been assumed that marsupials thrived in Australia because there were no competing terrestrial placental species, but the discovery of 115-million-year-old fossils with placental hallmarks suggests marsupials simply out-competed the early placentals.

By the time Australia split from Antarctica and began its long, lonely journey north, dinosaurs were extinct and flowering plants had taken over from conifers. The ancestors of kangaroos, koalas, possums and reptiles, as well as many bird species, were emerging – along with marsupial lions, primitive crocodiles and carnivorous kangaroos. Cut off from other land masses for the next 35 million years, these were to evolve in isolation, producing Australia's distinctive flora and fauna.

Until about 25 million years ago Australia was covered with rainforest but as it rafted north, it carried its cargo of plants and animals to a future which, thanks to climate change, was dramatically cooler and drier. Tough new sclerophyll plants, such as

Antarctic beech forests like this once covered much of Gondwana. (SM)

eucalypts, acacias and banksias, evolved from rainforest ancestors to suit new conditions. They were better adapted to drought and to infertile nitrogen- and phosphorous-poor soils. Also, as lightning strikes ignited increasing numbers of fires, they evolved not only to survive but even to promote a deadly force that gave them a competitive edge over ancestral, fire-sensitive forests. The new upstarts spread across the land and the rainforests retreated to moist pockets on the east coast. As drying continued, forests were replaced with woodlands and then with grasslands; by about two million years ago the inland had become desert. New types of kangaroo, which hopped, appeared alongside flesh-eating marsupials such as thylacines.

THE END OF ISOLATION

Common spotted cuscus. (KW/FLPA)

Bats had flown in over millennia but it was not until after Australia butted up against the Asian plate that the main wave of placental animals arrived. Rodents probably reached Australia from New Guinea and Indonesia either on rafts of vegetation or, as sea levels dropped, across newly exposed land bridges. Most, the 'old endemic' rodents (see page 64), arrived about four million years ago while the 'new endemics', the true rats, arrived less than one million years ago. Traffic was two-way. Fossil records suggest that cuscuses (a type of possum) evolved in Australia but, after spreading to New Guinea, died out in their original homeland, only to reappear when their descendants reinvaded. They didn't spread far and are today confined to the northern third of Queensland's Cape York Peninsula. The new placental arrivals would have found themselves in a land of giants: great herds of rhino-sized, wombat-like diprotodons; giant kangaroos, three times the size of today's 'big reds'; echidnas as big as sheep; marsupial tapirs; 7m-long lizards; 2.5m-long tortoises; 10m-long pythons; and 3m-high 'thunder birds' weighing 500kg. (One of these birds, a flesh-eater thought to be distantly related to waterfowl, has been nicknamed the 'Demon Duck of Doom'.) Most of this megafauna became extinct between about 40,000 and 20,000 years ago and debate rages as to the

8

cause. It may have been one or a combination of factors, including climate change, fire, and hunting by a particularly intelligent two-legged placental mammal that had also migrated to the continent from the north.

THRIVING THROUGH ADVERSITY

Life in Australia has evolved with adversity – impoverished soils, frequent fires and an erratic climate that swings between extended droughts and sudden floods in unpredictable cycles (see *Cycles of drought and flood*, page 17). As a consequence Australian animals have developed a range of intriguing survival strategies. They are both frugal and opportunistic. With limited resources many birds co-operate as families to raise young and the males of some dasyurid mammals are programmed to die soon after mating, thus reducing competition for food with their progeny. Energy is used economically. Koalas simply sleep a lot and move slowly when awake. Kangaroos hop, which is a more energy-efficient method of moving quickly than running (see page 44). Reproduction fluctuates according to resource availability. Some animals are very long-lived and procreate slowly, but many breed prolifically in the good times only to die off in large numbers when the going gets tough; female kangaroos even keep fertilised embryos in a state of suspended animation so macropod numbers boom quickly when good times follow droughts. Many animals, particularly birds, are nomadic, ready to respond to changing conditions, and huge numbers turn up when rare rains flood the inland. Sunshine is one resource that is available in Australia in particular abundance, and both plants and animals harness its energy. Where rainfall is also plentiful it fuels the fecund growth of tropical rainforests. Corals thrive where sunlight feeds the symbiotic plants within their tissues, and the greatest reptile diversity on the planet (coinciding with the world's greatest diversity of ants) occurs in the hottest, arid zones where conditions suit these solar-powered creatures well.

Kangaroos are well adapted to Australia's harsh conditions. (GL/FLPA)

THE HUMAN CONNECTION

The fruiting kapok tree (*Cochlospermum fraseri*), a calendar plant. (DW)

THE FIRST ARRIVALS

Somewhere between about 60,000 and 40,000 years ago, some island-hopping humans found their way to Australia from Java, Timor or New Guinea. They spread out across the continent, including Tasmania, and by the time of European settlement in 1788 up to 400 languages were spoken. Wild food was abundant and ideal for a semi-nomadic, hunter-gatherer lifestyle. Indeed, the Aboriginal diet was more varied and nutritious than that of many of the new arrivals at the time of European settlement. Living in societies based on complex rules, Aboriginal people existed in equilibrium with the land, intensely aware of natural cycles and moving according to seasonal availability of food. Calendar plants and animals provided cues: for example, fruiting kapok trees indicated the time to dig up turtle eggs, while particular insect calls meant it was time to harvest fruits in a distant part of the territory. They used fire as a management tool to clear pathways, flush out animals, stimulate fruiting and entice game to re-growth. Lengthy processing made poisonous foods edible, and by adding certain toxic plants to water they were able to stun and catch fishes. In a way that few outsiders can fully understand, Indigenous people felt – and still feel – profoundly and intimately connected to their tribal lands. They are part of their country and their country is part of them, a connection expressed in Dreamtime stories.

A different group of Indigenous people live on the islands in the Torres Strait, between Australia and New Guinea. Pursuing a traditional lifestyle that combines some agriculture with hunting and gathering, these seafaring people have strong links to the people of New Guinea and the Pacific.

Rock shelters have been decorated by generations of Aboriginal people. (SM)

Aboriginal people gathering bulbs and flowers on Cape York Peninsula. (KT)

Indigenous people saw many changes. The megafauna became extinct, volcanoes erupted and the climate changed. The last ice age was at its height about 22,000–20,000 years ago. Ice sheets covered Tasmania and – on the other side of the world – forced humans to retreat from the British Isles, so life in Australia must have been chilly. During the continent's driest periods, deserts covered larger areas than they do today and rainforests contracted to small refuges on moist mountain tops and protected gorges. Then, as the last ice age ended about 10,000 years ago, Australia's climate changed from cold and dry to hot and dry. Sea levels rose rapidly, covering large parts of the continental shelf, including the area currently occupied by the Great Barrier Reef. Grassy hunting plains disappeared underwater, transformed into 'sea country' territories of coastal tribes.

Indigenous people today, even in urban settings, proudly maintain a close, spiritual connection to their traditional country and, particularly in remote areas, still observe certain time-honoured laws. Collection of bush tucker (wild foods), fishing and hunting are still practised to some degree. For example, only Indigenous people can hunt dugongs and turtles, although modern pressures on these animals have necessitated some restrictions to preserve future stocks.

THE EUROPEAN INVASION

Indonesian, Portuguese, Spanish, Dutch and French sailors reached parts of Australia but the British, in 1788, were the first outsiders to settle. This was to have profound consequences for the flora and fauna, and the Indigenous people. Europeans treated Australia as a resource to be exploited: sealers and whalers devastated populations of marine mammals; miners flooded into any area that promised gold; timber-cutters came hard on their heels, felling forests; and huge areas were cleared for agriculture. Inappropriate farming practices, combined with a failure to understand the fragile and impoverished nature of Australia's soils and the climate's irregular cycle of droughts and floods (see page 17), have resulted in widespread environmental degradation and human hardship. Stripped of vegetation and eroded by the hard hooves of introduced livestock, many precious topsoils have been blown or washed away.

An anti-logging protest camp in Tasmania's Upper Florentine Valley. (DW)

CONSERVATION ISSUES

Australia has a woeful record of wildlife extinctions. Since 1788 over 115 plants and animals, including about 20 mammal, 23 bird and 4 frog species, have died out, thanks largely to habitat destruction, invasive species and the suppression of fire regimes traditionally practised by Indigenous people. In addition, over a thousand animals are listed as threatened.

Although much habitat destruction can be blamed on earlier generations, some continues today. Felling of old-growth forests is an issue that sees passionate conservationists setting up camps and tree-sits in the face of equally passionate opposition from frustrated loggers. (Old trees are immensely important to hollow-dwelling animals but, generally unsuitable for saw-logs, they are often reduced to low-value wood chips.) Sadly, these forests are often replaced with plantations of non-native trees, sprayed with dubious chemicals. Less obvious is the constant, piecemeal attrition of natural vegetation for agriculture and urban expansion.

INTRODUCED BULLIES

Since the arrival of the Europeans a huge number of plants and animals have been introduced from elsewhere, some accidentally, others for food, pest control, ornamentation, pets or comfort for homesick settlers. In the 1860s Acclimatisation Societies were established with the aim of introducing non-native animals, ranging from European songbirds to monkeys. The latter once played in the streets of Hobart, their introduction defended, '… for the amusement of the wayfarer who their gambols would delight as he lay under some gum-tree in the forest on a sultry day.' Although the monkeys eventually disappeared, many other species stayed on and multiplied, usually to the detriment of native animals and their habitats. After land clearing, weeds rank as the second greatest threat to biodiversity. In the form of trees, shrubs, vines, grasses and aquatic plants, they have invaded every habitat, smothering and crowding out native vegetation, choking wetlands, poisoning stock, excluding wild animals and spreading unnaturally hot fires.

Feral, introduced animals are no better. Foxes, released in the mid-1800s for recreational hunting, and cats (some of which may have arrived on Indonesian or Dutch ships before 1788) have been blamed for extinctions and near-extinctions of many native animals. A research team from the University of Canberra has estimated that the prey of feral cats amounts to 800,000 tonnes of small animals a year, and that doesn't include the victims of stray and domestic cats, or take account of the diseases that cats spread. Rabbits, also released for hunting, have stripped the land of ground cover, destroying food resources and shelter and contributing to the decline of many native animals, particularly in the vulnerable arid zone.

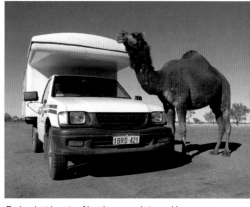

Redundant beasts of burden, camels turned loose are proliferating. (GZ/FLPA)

Meanwhile goats, horses, donkeys, buffaloes and cattle, with their hard hooves and voracious appetites, cause soil compaction, erosion and desertification, deprive native animals of essential shelter and destroy waterholes. Camels, too, deplete and foul watering points and overgraze vegetation. Feral pigs, thought to number 34 million, consume soil invertebrates, small vertebrates and native vegetation, spread weeds, degrade waterholes and have a serious potential to carry diseases such as foot-and-mouth. They also attract hunters and their dogs into environmentally sensitive areas. Cane toads (see page 127) poison a host of native terrestrial and aquatic animals; common (Indian) mynas compete aggressively with other birds and mammals for nesting hollows and food; non-native fishes eat, or outbreed, the locals; aggressive invasive ant species attack other animals; introduced starfish devastate shellfish … the list goes on.

WATER PRESSURES

Water is a precious commodity in Australia. Irrigation has allowed farmers to grow crops in unlikely places but this, too, has environmental costs. So much water from the Murray and Darling rivers is diverted for agriculture that very little now reaches the sea. This once mighty waterway is reduced in places to a muddy trickle plagued with salinity and toxic blue-green algal blooms. River red gums, denied regular floods, are dying – but these are just the more visible victims. The flows of many other rivers are also now regulated by dams, levees, tidal gates and channels, depriving aquatic animals of the natural pulses of flood and low flow with which they have evolved. Elsewhere, over-harvesting of groundwater is depriving plants and natural springs of invisible but essential sustenance.

Periodic droughts cause dams and reservoirs to shrink. (CC/FLPA)

An unanticipated effect of irrigation and vegetation clearing has been the development of soil salinity. Unbeknown to early farmers, large amounts of salt had been lying below the surface for millennia but, as they replaced native vegetation with shallow-rooted crops and pastures, and established irrigation, water tables rose, bringing the salt to the surface and releasing it into waterways. Not only does this render the land infertile but it also corrodes structures such as buildings and roads. An estimated 5.7 million hectares are affected and this is expected to rise to 17 million hectares by 2050.

Neither are the oceans immune. Sediment, fertiliser, chemical and general pollution run-off from agriculture and from settled areas is affecting water quality and promoting excessive algal growth. This includes phytoplankton on the water surface, which has been blamed for the increased survival of excessive numbers of larvae of the crown-of-thorns starfish, a major predator of coral. Overfishing, destruction of mangrove fish nurseries and damage to the sea floor by trawlers, as well as the wastefully discarded bycatch (up to ten times the weight of prawns harvested) all threaten biodiversity.

PUTTING IT RIGHT

The good news is that, with the low population density and vast size, Australia's human footprint is relatively light compared with that of most parts of the world. Over 10% of the land surface is within protected areas and this proportion is growing. In addition to government-controlled national parks, independent organisations are buying up environmentally significant land and, increasingly, people are entering into conservation agreements on private property. Australia has over 65 Ramsar sites (wetlands of international importance), covering more than seven million hectares, and 15 World Heritage Sites listed for natural values.

Lessons from the past have been learned. Environmental issues, and sustainability, are now of mainstream concern. The trend is to be more cautious when tampering with ecosystem integrity and to tap into traditional Indigenous knowledge. Some steps are being taken to repair the damage. Native vegetation is being replanted and water allocations to farmers are being reviewed and reduced, allowing 'environmental flows' to reinvigorate rivers. Salt-tolerant trees are being planted to combat salinity.

A Bennett's wallaby finds refuge on private land in Tasmania. (DW)

Steps are being taken to control weeds and feral animals, although with mixed results. The dense populations of swamp buffalo (*Bubalus bubalis*) that once caused widespread destruction of northern wetlands have been intensively culled. However, eradications, like the original introductions, can have unintended consequences: when cats on remote Macquarie Island were successfully removed in order to save nesting seabirds, rabbit numbers soared, damaging vegetation and exposing penguins to predators. Removal must therefore be done with care. On the mainland, conversely, the removal of rabbits may leave foxes, cats and other predators to target even more native animals. Rehabilitation, unfortunately, has a long way to go.

CLIMATE

Australia is the driest inhabited continent. Much of the moisture from prevailing southeasterly trade winds falls as rain on the eastern side of the Great Dividing Range, with most of the rest of the continent – 70% of which is classed as arid – receiving less than 500mm and often less than 250mm in an average year. This arid zone stretches to the west and mid-southern coasts. Summer days, from about October to March, are searingly hot in the centre but winter months are pleasantly warm during the day, with temperatures sometimes falling below freezing at night.

Low rainfall supports sparse woodland across much of Australia. (GW)

Tully's giant gumboot. (SM)

Life in the northern tropics, an arc stretching from east to west across the continent, is dominated by a summer wet season (December to March approximately) and a winter dry season (May to October). In summer the monsoon trough migrates south of the Equator, inundating the landscape. Cyclones periodically make landfall along the tropical coasts at this time, bringing strong winds and torrential rainfall that may penetrate quite far inland. The tropical north Queensland coast, east of the Great Dividing Range, receives rain from both the monsoon and the southeasterlies, making it the wettest part of Australia. The towns of Tully and Babinda each receive over 4,000mm a year and compete for the annual Golden Gumboot wettest town award. Tully holds the overall record: 7,900mm of rain in 1950, represented by a giant 7.9m gumboot statue in the town. Summer temperatures are usually around 30–35°C but humidity is extremely high, making life very uncomfortable. During the dry season, from May to October, the Queensland coast receives much less rain (especially August to October) and the savanna region virtually none. Skies are usually clear, and temperatures and humidity are lower; winter is the best time to visit the north.

Coastal New South Wales has a sunny, temperate climate. Minimum temperatures rarely drop below 10°C in Sydney and the summer average maximum is about 25°C – though it can exceed 40°C during summer heatwaves. Most rain falls in the first half of the year. The southern and southwestern coast of the mainland has a Mediterranean-type climate,

Snow in Tasmania's Cradle Mountain-Lake St Clair National Park. (SN)

with hot, dry summers and cool winters. Summer temperatures often fluctuate suddenly, depending on whether winds are blowing from the scorching interior or from the Antarctic. They can exceed 45°C and then, within hours, drop by 10–20°C. Most rain falls between May and August, particularly on higher ground. It is associated with westerly winds and winter depressions, a spin-off from a vortex of winds circling the Antarctic continent. However, the southern states are subject to prolonged droughts that leave the landscape parched and highly combustible.

Tasmania, surrounded by sea, does not experience extremes and has pleasantly warm summers. It receives rain throughout the year, most falling in the west. Snow falls on higher parts of Tasmania and on the alpine region of Victoria and New South Wales where it supports a skiing industry. Patches persist all year in sheltered spots.

CYCLES OF DROUGHT AND FLOOD

Australian weather systems are affected by a pattern that is not dictated by annual seasons but marches to the beat of a different climatic drum. Trade winds normally push warm water across the Pacific towards Australia, creating moist air which rises and produces rain. If these winds weaken, the system can go into reverse, causing drought in Australia but bringing rain to South America, where the phenomenon has been named *El Niño*, or the Boy Child, since it becomes apparent about Christmas. It is measured, and predicted, by the Southern Oscillation Index (SOI), based on differences in air pressure between Tahiti and Darwin. The SOI is often included in weather reports and there are concerns that climate change will increase the number of *El Niño* (drought) years. *La Niña*, the Girl Child, occurs when the normal situation is exaggerated and good rains fall in Australia. Although farmers, geared to annual cycles, have difficulty adapting to this irregular pattern, native wildlife tends to be well attuned, adjusting breeding according to conditions.

Wet season clouds loom over tropical north Queensland's Tyto Wetlands. (SM)

More destructive weather, like 2006's cyclone Larry, is anticipated. (SM)

CHANGING CLIMATE

The effects of global climate change are already apparent in Australia. Coral bleaching, a serious threat to the Great Barrier Reef, has become much more frequent and widespread in recent decades (see *Corals and bleaching*, page 145). Southern Australia, including Tasmania, has been hammered by excessively long droughts and unprecedented heatwaves that have seen tinder-dry forests savaged by ferocious bushfires. It is thought that global warming is causing the circumpolar wind vortex to shrink, depriving southern fringes of much needed rain. Recent research also suggests that it is interfering with an interaction between the Indian and Pacific oceans that should normally bring moisture to the western side of the continent, flowing through to Victoria. Meanwhile northern regions have suffered from unusually large floods.

Scientists anticipate extreme weather events in future, including more, and increasingly intense, cyclones. The northeastern mountain tops, which sheltered flora and fauna through the harshest periods in Australia's climatic history, are expected to become drier, leaving animals for which they are a last refuge with nowhere higher to climb. At the southern end of the Great Dividing Range alpine meadows are already losing species, and it is feared that reduced, protective snow cover will drive the mountain pygmy possum to extinction. Flowering, fruiting and breeding cycles are already showing signs of disruption. While this is a global phenomenon, Australians can take their share of the blame as producers of among the world's highest per capita greenhouse gas emissions; the country is a major user – and exporter – of coal.

WEATHERPERSON-SPEAK DOWNUNDER

In Britain a 'mild' day is a pleasantly warm one; in Australia it is pleasantly cool. British forecasters announce a rainy day with regret; in Australia 'good falls' are reported with a note of triumph; precipitation is a national obsession as farmers grapple with extended droughts that are expected to get worse with climate change. It is a land of extremes. In one November weekend when Cairns temperatures exceeded 36°C, parts of the Australian Alps received a thick blanket of snow.

HABITATS

Subtropical rainforest in
Queensland's Lamington
National Park. (SN)

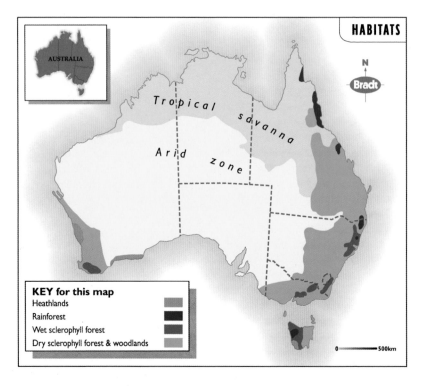

KEY for this map
Heathlands
Rainforest
Wet sclerophyll forest
Dry sclerophyll forest & woodlands

0 ———— 500km

THE ARID ZONE

Seventy per cent of Australia is classified as arid. Stretching from the Great Dividing Range right to the coast of Western Australia and through the Nullabor Plain to the south coast, much of this zone receives a median annual rainfall of less than 200mm. Soils, derived from ancient sandstone and limestone, are poor – yet this area is far from lifeless.

Spinifex in Purnululu National Park, Western Australia. (SN)

THE DESERTS

True, barren deserts – dunefields and stony deserts, the latter covered with small, polished stones known as 'gibbers' – are limited to parts of the Simpson, Great Victoria and Great Sandy deserts. More typically the landscape is one of red earth dotted with drought and salt-resistant bluebushes (*Maireana* spp), saltbushes (*Atriplex* spp) and hummock grasses (*Triodia* spp). These hardy grasses, commonly known as spinifex, are endemic to Australia and cover about a quarter of the continent. Dome-shaped, spiky clumps spread out as they age, creating 'doughnut' rings with dead centres.

The leaves, tightly rolled to minimise moisture loss, form spikes that can make bushwalking a painful experience. However, they also protect a large number of animals, including a remarkable diversity of reptiles. Resin in the leaves, which was traditionally used as glue, causes them to burn fiercely. The plant erupts in a ball of flames but soon re-sprouts or regenerates from seed.

Irregular rains bring boom times. Masses of flowers blossom and nomadic birds arrive to feed on nectar, seeds and insects. Populations of mammals such as hopping-mice increase rapidly. This fuels, in turn, an irruption of raptors and other predators. When the feast is over, animals die or move on, leaving residents such as wrens, lizards and the hardiest mammals to eke out an existence through the dry times. Fires, too, provide a bonanza – in the form of fleeing animals for predators and, later, fresh growth for grazers.

THE RIVERS AND EPHEMERAL WETLANDS

The arid zone is criss-crossed with dry watercourses. These only rarely fill with water, thanks usually to rain that fell hundreds of kilometres away. Having travelled for weeks, this water rolls along bone-dry riverbeds bearing foam and accumulated debris. Progress can be as slow as walking pace as the front soaks into the sand but, within minutes, an empty riverbed is occupied by flowing water. Desert rivers, instead of reaching the sea, feed swamps, billabongs and ephemeral salt- and freshwater lakes, stimulating explosions of life. Vast numbers of tiny crustaceans and molluscs hatch from eggs, some produced more than 20 years earlier and dispersed by wind. Not only are these eggs drought-resistant but they may actually require a period of desiccation in order to develop. This bounty feeds native fishes, crustaceans and frogs, and draws huge numbers of nomadic birds – stilts, avocets, cormorants, ibises and pelicans – inland to breed. After weeks, months or years the water eventually evaporates. It may be decades before the rivers flow again.

River red gums line a dry desert riverbed. (SM)

River red gums (*Eucalyptus camaldulensis*) line many watercourses. These magnificent, branching trees, named for their red timber, have a mainly white bark. Living for perhaps a thousand years, a river red gum can grow to 45m in height, with a root system of almost equal size hidden below the ground. These deep roots suck up water, allowing the tree to survive long periods between drinks and to withstand raging floodwaters when they arrive. This tree's habit of suddenly dropping large branches has given it the nickname 'widow-maker'. The resulting hollows, however, make valuable nests and roosts for birds – especially parrots – as well as bats, possums and other animals. Insects feed on the leaves, ants on the seeds, beetles on the sap and termites on the timber – each of these providing, in turn, food for other animals. Small wonder then that the river red gum is also known as 'nature's boarding house'. The coolibah (*E. coolabah*) is another tree of arid-zone rivers and floodplains. Since its seeds will not germinate without being immersed in water, it is restricted to places that are periodically flooded.

Desert ranges and woodland, Kata Tjuta, Northern Territory. (SM)

WOODLANDS

Vegetation in the arid zone can vary within short distances, from low shrubland to quite dense woodland, according to subtle changes in soil type, water availability or protection from bushfires. Low woodland, with sparse trees, is widespread. Desert oaks (*Allocasuarina decaisneana*) can form groves in deep sand. Despite their Christmas tree appearance they are actually flowering plants. Their foliage, like that of all casuarinas, resembles pine needles, but is actually composed of narrow branches with whorls of tiny, scale-like leaves encircling each joint.

Australia's commonest tree, the mulga (*Acacia aneura*), is found across 20% of the mainland, often in dense groves. It is adapted to nutrient-poor soils and can survive on as little as 50mm rainfall a year. Its leaf-like phyllodes (see *The wattle: the national flower*, page 23) are held vertically to minimise exposure to the midday sun, and to channel any rain or dew down the branches to the roots. Branching from just above ground level, it can grow as a low shrub or up to 15m in height. This very important tree had many traditional uses: hard timber for tools and firewood; seeds, galls and lerp insects (see page 137) for food; branches for shelters; and bark and leaves for medicines.

Mulga parrots (*Psephotus varius*) inhabit mulga and mallee woodlands. (IM)

The witchetty bush (*A. kempeana*) looks like a shrubby mulga with broader phyllodes. It is the source of witchetty grubs, large moth larvae that feed inside the roots and are a favourite Aboriginal food, eaten uncooked (they are said to resemble raw egg) or baked in the fire. Different witchetty grubs – moth and beetle larvae – are found in different plants.

22

WATTLE: THE NATIONAL FLOWER

With over 900 species, acacias comprise Australia's largest genus of flowering plants. They are commonly known as wattles, because early European settlers used the thin branches, woven together, as the framework for wattle-and-daub (mud) structures. The yellow blossoms of the golden wattle (*Acacia pycnantha*) have been adopted as the national flower; Wattle Day is celebrated on 1 September each year and Australian sporting teams often wear green and gold to represent wattle 'leaves' and flowers. In fact, most adult acacias have no leaves, relying on green flattened, or needle-like, leaf stalks known as phyllodes, for photosynthesis. This decreases water loss, a useful strategy as wattles typically grow where rainfall is too low to sustain eucalypts. The phyllodes also contain chemicals to deter herbivores but produce nectar to attract ants, which, in turn, attack herbivorous insects.

Acacias are legumes, so they supplement their meagre income from impoverished soils by harnessing bacteria in their roots to fix nitrogen from the air. They also employ ants to sow their seeds. These seeds are hard and ant-proof (otherwise they would be eaten), but each has a nutritious appendage (elaiosome) attached. The ants carry them into their underground nests where they feed on the elaiosomes and discard the seeds, which lie dormant until a bushfire stimulates them to germinate (see *The role of fire*, page 35). Australian acacias are very different to African acacias. African acacias have more conventional leaves. They also produce nutritious seed pods to attract large mammals, which disperse the seeds, fertilise the trees with their droppings and remove or trample down fire-attracting grasses that surround the tree.

Mallee is the term used for a group of over one hundred *Eucalyptus* and *Corymbia* tree species that produce multiple stems instead of a single trunk. Mallee shrubland requires rather more rainfall than mulga and dominates a band across southern Australia and right into the centre – although large areas have now been cleared for agriculture. Most are short – less than 10m high – and, like all eucalypts, they are very hardy. Long lateral roots store water, an important resource for Aboriginal people; a 5m length of red mallee (*E. eucentrica*) root, removed from the ground and upended to drain, can produce a bucket of drinking water.

RANGES

Rust-red ranges and rocky outcrops, decorated with elegant white-barked ghost gums (*Corymbia aparrerinja*), incised with deep chasms and harbouring tranquil waterholes, are a haven for wildlife in the arid zone. Offering shade,

Desert waterhole in Trephina Gorge Nature Park, near Alice Springs. (SM)

Desert ranges shelter black-footed rock-wallabies. (SM)

moisture and protection from bushfires, many gorges are refuges for relict plant species, such as cycads, *Livistona* palms and ferns, which were once widespread when Australia's climate was wetter. Rock-wallabies, bats and other animals shelter in these sanctuaries. Rainfall, absorbed by sandstone, trickles through and reappears, sometimes over a hundred years later, to feed permanent springs and pools supporting fishes, frogs, ducks and many other creatures. These miraculous oases, set in the often harsh outback landscape, are among Australia's most special places.

SURVIVAL STRATEGIES IN THE ARID ZONE

The flora and fauna of the arid zone have to be tough to survive. It has been suggested that some plants may be relict mangroves, dating back to the days of the inland sea, and have simply adapted water-conserving strategies from salty to drought conditions. Small, narrow leaves are angled away from the sun and thick, waxy coatings, hairs or reflective surfaces minimise water loss. Such plants also employ a range of strategies to survive fire (see *The role of fire*, page 35).

Many animals retreat into burrows to avoid the daytime heat and most are extremely frugal with water. Carnivores and insectivores may obtain enough moisture from their prey, but some mammalian seed-eaters have developed ultra-efficient kidneys and, like reptiles and birds, concentrate their urine, excreting it as a white drop of uric acid; the spinifex hopping mouse has the most concentrated urine of any mammal. They may also store fat in their tails for lean times. Reptiles thrive in the arid zone, sunshine fuelling their activity. Birds, with mobility on their side, may be migratory or nomadic, appearing when conditions are good and then moving on. Animals are good at keeping themselves hidden but plentiful raptors in the skies are an indication that, for the observant, there is ample life to be found in the arid zone.

Centralian blue-tongued skink. (GW)

Massive termite mounds are characteristic of northern Australia's savannas. (SN)

TROPICAL SAVANNA

Tropical savannas are grasslands with scattered trees that sometimes form woodlands with a grassy understorey. This habitat occupies one-quarter of the mainland, forming a vast band across the north, west of the Great Dividing Range. It has been called a desert where it rains three months of the year, and life here is dominated by an annual cycle of summer monsoon floods and winter drought and fire. Some of Australia's most iconic areas – Kakadu National Park, the Kimberley and Cape York Peninsula – fall in this zone.

TROPICAL WOODLANDS

About 70–80% of the savanna belt is covered with tropical woodland. Dry, sandy, leached soils are generally too infertile to support dense growth so, unlike forests, where the crowns touch, the trees are well spaced with an understorey of shrubs and grasses. Wiry eucalypt species dominate, with wizened, crevassed barks and tough names like ironwood, stringybark and bloodwood. They have deep roots and thick barks to conserve water and survive the fires that rip through during the dry season. Deciduous species save moisture by dropping their leaves at this time. Common understorey plants include cycads (Cycadales) – ancient, leathery-leafed, palm-like plants that predate flowering species – and grass trees (*Xanthorrhoea* spp) with mops of spiky leaves. Both burn readily but grow back with fresh, green crowns.

Termite mounds stud the landscape, and emus and Australian bustards stalk through grasses that can grow 3m high. About 55 of Australia's 90-plus seed-eating birds, including parrots, pigeons, quails and 14 of the18 native finch species, are found here. The woodlands are also home to wallabies and kangaroos, as well as bandicoots, dingoes, monitor lizards and other reptiles. Common tree snakes are a regular sight and frilled lizards descend from the trees during the wet season. Arboreal mammals (chiefly possums and gliders) spend their days in tree hollows and emerge at night. Eucalypt, grevillea and

25

acacia blossoms attract insects, flying-foxes, honeyeaters and other birds. Flocks of raucous red-tailed black-cockatoos, sometimes thousands strong, are especially obvious in the dry season. Numerous raptors patrol the skies, black kites circling fires to pick up fleeing animals.

Moister conditions allow denser rainforests (see *Monsoon and dry rainforests*, page 29) to develop. Gallery forests line rivers, standing out as ribbons of green winding through the sparse woodland. Other patches occur where a subtle combination of topography, soils, climate and protection from fire provides favourable conditions.

Dense greenery hugs savanna river courses. (SM)

WETLANDS

The wet season transforms the savanna landscape. Rivers burst out of their banks and spread across the countryside, filling ephemeral floodplains with a sheet of water. This is bonanza time for wildlife. Lilies, rushes and wild rice sprout. Fishes, frogs and freshwater turtles multiply, feeding a host of reptiles and birds. Only some plants can tolerate having their roots submerged in water. Large, shady, paperbark trees (*Melaleuca* spp) grow in low-lying areas, which soon become swamps. Their thick, papery bark protects the trees from moisture loss and fire in the dry season; the scientific name means 'black white', referring

Savanna billabongs, here in Kakadu National Park, are a magnet for wildlife. (IM)

to its appearance after fire. This bark peels off easily and was used traditionally for roofing shelters. Nectar-rich, bottlebrush-type flowers are very attractive to insects, birds and flying-foxes. There are nearly 300 *Melaleuca* species, most of them endemic to Australia, some growing as shrubs or trees in open woodland. *Pandanus* trees are common in paperbark swamps. Prop roots around the trunk help to support a dense crown of strap-like, saw-edged leaves – a safe haven for many animals – and heavy, pineapple-like fruits. The leaves are an important source of materials for making traditional baskets and mats.

As the wetlands dry out, insects feeding on rotting vegetation fuel breeding cycles of ducks. Isolated river bends become billabongs filled with lotus and waterlily flowers and swamps become cracked mud. The ever-shrinking waters draw great concentrations of waterbirds, notably magpie-geese and whistling-ducks. Increasing heat and humidity encourage crocodiles to move around and prepare to breed. Lightning strikes start fires, clouds roll in and then the inundation begins again.

Blue-winged kookaburras are common in savanna woodlands. (IM)

FORESTS

RAINFORESTS

Australia's rainforests are a legacy of ancient times, when they spread right across Gondwana. Restricted to moist pockets on the east coast, they now cover just 0.3% of the continent. Nonetheless, they support about half of all the country's plant families and about half of bird and a third of mammal species, some of which share their Gondwanan ancestry.

Rainforest typically has a closed canopy and grows in areas of plentiful rainfall. It takes many forms, varying with latitude, altitude, aspect, soil type and climate – particularly rainfall. Some rainforests persist as small isolated pockets but most form a complex mosaic, subtle differences in conditions dictating which type prevails as one merges into another or into neighbouring vegetation types.

Competition among rainforest plants is not for water but for sunlight. Trees stretch tall on straight trunks, spreading their crowns and creating an aerial mat of overlapping, sun-hungry leaves that shades everything below. Some plants employ different strategies for reaching the light. Epiphytic ferns and orchids, and parasitic mistletoes, squat on high branches and trunks – wherever their seeds germinated. Vines twist, twine or hitch their way up on hooked tendrils. Modest forest floor plants, such as ferns and gingers, stack their leaves with chlorophyll to make maximum use of the few flecks of sunlight that come their way. Saplings, too, live in this dark zone, biding their time for 20 years or more, waiting for a tree fall to open up the canopy. Energy, in the form of light, then fuels a race, the fastest saplings winning the coveted place in the sun.

Tropical rainforest in Daintree National Park, Queensland. (SN)

Tropical and subtropical rainforests

These are the most complex types of rainforest, flourishing in warm, consistently wet conditions. The largest tract, the Wet Tropics World Heritage Area, covers a 450km strip between Cooktown and Townsville in north Queensland. Boasting over 3,000 plant species, it benefits not just from high temperatures and monsoonal downpours in summer, but also regular rainfall in winter from southeast trade winds. Other rainforest stands grow further north, in the Iron and McIlwraith ranges, and, where conditions are suitable, south along the eastern Great Dividing Range to the vicinity of Sydney.

In optimum conditions these forests are multi-layered, 20–45m high, and harbour a bewildering diversity of interwoven and interacting plant and animal species. The theme is green. Leaves tend to be large and there are numerous woody vines, epiphytes and palms, including the scrambling rattan palm (*Calamus* spp), known as lawyer cane or wait-a-while because passers-by are so often caught by its hooks. Many of the trees have extensive buttresses – narrow flanges at the trunk base that are thought to help stabilise these shallow-rooted giants and/or help them breathe when waterlogged. Some trees produce fruit directly from trunks and branches, a strategy for attracting pollinators living below the canopy.

Black flying-foxes frequent northern forests and woodlands. (IM)

Strangler figs (*Ficus* spp) grow into living sculptures. A seed germinates high on another tree and the young fig sends roots down to the ground. Gradually these coalesce around the host tree's trunk, out-competing it for water and nutrients at ground level while vigorous branches block out light in the canopy. The host eventually dies and rots away, leaving a hollow in the centre of the fig that grows on to become a forest giant.

Tropical rainforests support a huge range of animals. Among the birds, grey-headed robins, Lewin's honeyeaters and catbirds – with their distinctive calls – are some of the most obvious, while fruit-eating pigeons and parrots feed in the canopy and mid-storey and Australian brush-turkeys are conspicuous on the forest floor. Other ground-dwelling birds – noisy pittas, whipbirds, logrunners, chowchillas, cassowaries (in northern forests) and lyrebirds (in southern forests) – are more secretive. Pademelons, musky rat-kangaroos (in the north) and bandicoots also fossick in the leaf-litter under the watchful gaze of forest dragons. Flying-foxes arrive at night, sharing the treetops with leaf-eating possums, pythons, giant white-tailed rats and their relatives.

Monsoon and dry rainforests

Dry rainforests grow in northern and eastern Australia, in situations protected from fire but subject to seasonal droughts. Although less diverse, with a high proportion of deciduous

Buff-breasted paradise-kingfishers visit northeastern rainforests in summer. (IM)

trees, they share with other rainforests a closed, if sparse, canopy and abundant woody vines. These forests usually have just two tree layers, with tall emergents, such as hoop pines (*Araucaria cunninghamii*), looming over thorny shrubs. Surrounded by drier vegetation, this dense tangle of growth provides welcome shade. Flying-foxes and birds – pigeons, fruit-doves, orioles and figbirds – flock to these havens to feast on fruit, playing a vital role in maintaining small forest patches by dispersing seeds between them. Fig trees are prominent. Their fruits are actually inside-out flowers; stigmas and stamens are contained within the fruit and are pollinated by specialised wasps that burrow inside to lay their eggs. Littoral rainforests, found on warm, moist coastal areas, combine features of subtropical and dry rainforests.

Temperate rainforests

Warm temperate rainforests are simpler versions of subtropical rainforests, growing on poorer soils and higher (thus cooler) altitudes in New South Wales and parts of eastern Victoria. Typically they have a double-layered canopy, composed of 3–15 slender-trunked species, often dominated by coachwood (*Ceratopetalum apetalum*) and sassafras (*Doryphora sassafras*). The leaves are fairly small and there are thin, wiry vines and epiphytes growing among the trees, but few palms.

Cool temperate rainforests occur in cool areas, with high rainfall and mists, from high altitudes on the Queensland–New South Wales border to low altitudes in parts of Tasmania. Usually just one or two species, with numerous small leaves, form an even

Mossy Antarctic beech forests, once widespread, are restricted to small pockets, here in Queensland's Lamington National Park. (SN)

canopy. Antarctic beech (*Nothofagus moorei*) predominates in the north; myrtle beech (*N. cunninghamii*) in Victoria and Tasmania. Their massive, gnarled, moss-covered trunks lend these ancient Gondwanan forests a primordial atmosphere. An Antarctic beech can be several thousand years old because, as the main trunk dies, secondary stems arise from its base. Ferns, mosses, lichens, liverworts and fungi flourish in these magical forests, covering trunks and rocks and hanging from branches.

SCLEROPHYLL FORESTS AND WOODLANDS

Sclerophyll vegetation dominates Australia. The word, derived from Greek, means 'hard leaf' and describes the tough, water-conserving foliage found on eucalypts, acacias, banksias, bottlebrushes, grevilleas, hakeas and other plants so characteristic of the Australian bush. These leaves contain chemicals to discourage herbivores but, as some are highly flammable oils, sclerophyll plants need to contend with frequent bushfires (see *The role of fire*, page 35). Although this vegetation type is frequently sparse and shrubby, some of the country's most magnificent forests are composed of eucalypts. One of the keys to their success is a symbiotic relationship with mycorrhizal fungi. These fungi surround the roots of the trees, tapping into their hosts' food supply, but repay this by feeding back water, and elements such as nitrogen and phosphorous. The fine fungal filaments are able to penetrate tiny spaces, essentially extending the underground reach of the tree. Animals are also involved. Over 40 mammal species feed on the underground fungal fruiting bodies – truffles – and disperse the spores; some bettongs and potoroos, dubbed 'truffle junkies', feed on little else.

THE UBIQUITOUS EUCALYPT

It is the quintessential Australian experience – the distinctive scent of sun-roasted eucalypt trees under a piercing blue sky. Evolution shaped these trees especially for the Australian environment. Of the 900 or so species (if *Angophora* and contentiously separated *Corymbia* species are included) just a few grow naturally elsewhere, having spread north to adjacent islands at times of low sea levels. The vast majority of eucalypts call Australia home and a large number of Australian animals reside in their hollows and branches.

Eucalypts come in many guises. Classic smooth-barked gum trees shed a thin layer of outermost bark every year, but others, such as ironbarks, stringybarks, peppermints and boxes, have thick, solid, rough or spongy barks. Many species exude gum in response to injury; bloodwoods are named for the red colour of their oozing juices.

A eucalypt is built for survival. Roots are deep, with fungal associates extending their reach even further. Tough leaves, with sunken stomata, are designed to minimise water loss and, hanging sideways to the sun, avoid excessive exposure. When they have done their duty, their nutrients are thriftily withdrawn before they are allowed to drop. Seeds are protected inside woody gum nuts and flowers develop under a woody cap made from fused petals, a feature encoded in the name: 'eucalyptus', derived from Greek, means 'well covered'. These trees are prepared for the worst. If damaged by fire, drought, storm or insect attack they are ready to reshoot from trunks or from underground tubers, or to broadcast seeds (see *The role of fire*, page 35).

Moth larvae create distinctive tracks on scribbly gum trunks. (SM)

Wet sclerophyll forests

Like columns of a marvellous, living cathedral, the uniformly straight trunks of mountain ash (*Eucalyptus regnans*) soar up to a canopy 60m or more above the forest floor. This tree is the tallest flowering plant in the world. Some living specimens have been measured at about 90m but reports from the 1870s suggest specimens of well over 100m, even up to 150m, existed at the time of European settlement, topping even the giant redwoods (non-flowering conifers) of North America.

Wet sclerophyll forests are dominated by eucalypts. Known also as 'tall, open forests', they have a more open canopy than rainforests and stand above a dense understorey of small trees, shrubs and, in moister places, tree ferns. They usually occupy areas with high

31

Mountain ash trees loom over fern gullies in Victoria's Dandenong Ranges. (SM)

rainfall, between rainforest and dry sclerophyll. In north Queensland this strip is less than one kilometre wide in places, but more extensive stands grow further south. In the north rose gums (*E. grandis*) – known as flooded gums elsewhere – are common. Around the southern parts of the Great Dividing Range and Tasmania, mountain ash (called swamp ash in Tasmania) predominates, with alpine ash (*E. delegatensis*) on higher slopes. Western Australia's tall forests are composed of locally endemic species – karri (*E. diversicolor*), which rivals mountain ash in height, and massive red and yellow tingle trees (*E. jacksonii; E. guilfoylei*).

These forests have a phoenix-like relationship with fire. Trees, such as mountain ash, die if burned but, paradoxically, rely on fire to procreate. Young trees need light and cannot become established unless the dense understorey is removed. In their final moments, as the parent trees burn, capsules in the canopy shower the ground with freshly liberated seeds (up to 14 million per hectare). With understorey competition destroyed, saplings sprout up between the skeletons of the parent trees. However, these trees may not mature for 20 years or more so if they are burnt before they can produce seed they are in danger of becoming locally extinct. Alternatively, if a forest is never burned, the trees are in danger of dying of old age without being replaced and neighbouring rainforest may then take over. Areas may fluctuate between these two forest types according to fire regimes.

Some animals are wholly or largely dependent on these forests. Older trees, which have dropped limbs and been scarred by fire over hundreds of years, develop holes and hollows. These provide essential shelter for a great number of animals, from possums, gliders and birds, to reptiles, frogs and invertebrates. Dependent species include the yellow-bellied glider and Leadbeater's possum (*Gymnobelideus leadbeateri*), an endangered species from a tiny part of Victoria that depends on hollows in mountain ash trees at least 200 years old. Among the birds, bell miners can be abundant, treecreepers are common and superb lyrebirds may inhabit the understorey.

Dry sclerophyll forests

Where conditions are less favourable dry sclerophyll forests take over, eventually merging into sclerophyll woodlands. These cover extensive areas of the southeastern and southwestern mainland, and eastern Tasmania. A number of tree species combine to form a fairly even canopy, 25–35m high, which is open enough to allow the growth of grasses and shrubs. After fire, many species re-sprout from epicormic shoots and lignotubers (see *The role of fire*, page 35). Many of the best-known Australian animals inhabit dry sclerophyll forests and their neighbouring woodlands, including koalas, grey kangaroos, common wombats, echidnas, possums, gliders and emus.

Dry sclerophyll woodlands

With increasing aridity and decreasing soil fertility, forests gradually become woodlands. Trees are shorter and more widely spaced, with an open canopy.

Remnant box-ironwood woodland in Victoria's Chiltern-Mount Pilot National Park. (SM)

These woodlands take many different forms, from the snow gums of alpine regions to isolated stands of trees in moister parts of the arid interior and vast tracts of the northern savannas (see *Tropical woodlands*, page 25). They cover much of Australia but, since European settlement, huge areas have been taken over for stock and crops, particularly in the temperate, winter rainfall areas of the southeast and southwest. Sometimes just small pockets of the original vegetation have been belatedly protected, providing a last stronghold for animal species such as the numbat in Western Australia, and regent honeyeater (*Xanthomyza phrygia*) and turquoise parrot (*Neophema pulchella*) in the southeast.

HEATHLANDS

Heathlands are found along coastlines and at high altitudes, where they thrive on adversity. Soils derived from sand, sandstone or granite are thin, acidic and infertile, and plants here may be subjected to drought, fire, cold, strong wind, salt or swampy conditions. Typically the ground is covered with a dense, stunted shrub layer, less than 2m high, dominated by teatree (*Leptospermum* spp), grass tree, banksia and other sclerophyll species. Flamboyant arrays of flowering plants, rich in nectar, provide food and shelter for a host of animals. Resident birds, including ground parrots (*Pezoporus wallicus*), southern emu-wrens (*Stipiturus malachurus*) and bristlebirds, are joined periodically by visiting nectar-feeding species.

Kwongan heathlands are a global biodiversity hotspot. (SM)

On the infertile alpine soils sundews trap insects for nutrition. (SM)

The heathlands of Western Australia are the most diverse and are considered a biodiversity hotspot of global significance. Known as kwongan – the local Aboriginal name for 'sandy plain' – they grow on some of the poorest soils in the continent. It is believed that soil infertility is the key to this diversity. No single species is able to dominate. Instead, numerous species (from relatively few families) have evolved, each adapted to a particular, specialised niche or microhabitat. Included are over 300 types of terrestrial orchid and numerous carnivorous plants, notably sundews (*Drosera* spp), which obtain essential nutrients from insect prey. Flowering plants compete with each other to attract pollinators such as honey possums, honeyeaters and insects; providing nectar to keep them alive in a nutrient-poor environment is a sound investment. To lure pollinators several orchid flowers mimic the shape and smell of female wasps so convincingly that the male wasps attempt to mate with them and, having been dusted with pollen, go on to repeat their mistake with other orchids in the neighbourhood.

Buttongrass moorland covers poorly drained parts of the southeastern mainland and large parts of Tasmania. Actually a sedge, buttongrass (*Gymnoschoenus sphaerocephalus*) produces long stalks with button-like flower heads. It provides important shelter and food for many animals, from wombats to wrens, frogs and burrowing crayfishes. Like many heathland plants buttongrass burns readily; occasional fires are important for maintaining the diversity of these habitats.

In altitudes above 1,800m in the alpine area of southeastern Australia, where even hardy snow gums cannot survive prolonged snow cover, alpine herbfields and tussocks support over 200 species of low-growing plant. While some are dormant in winter, others have a natural anti-freeze. Protected under the snow, they quickly put on a show of flowers when it melts. Mountain pygmy possums are also protected under the snow, living off fat gained when feasting on bogong moths during summer months.

Dry season fires in the savanna region are frequent natural events. (KT)

THE ROLE OF FIRE

As Victoria's bushfires in early 2009 so tragically demonstrated, Australia is one of the most bushfire-prone parts of the planet. Much of its flora has evolved to harness this dynamic force. Eucalypts not only create kindling, in the form of dropped branches and peeling bark but, thanks to their volatile oils, are also inherently flammable. Many banksias, grass trees, cycads, acacias, hakeas, casuarinas, orchids and grasses survive, and even thrive on, occasional fire. Some native orchids only blossom after being burnt, while grass trees and waratahs are stimulated to flower particularly profusely. These plants have developed a range of survival strategies.

SEEDERS AND SPROUTERS

Some plants are seeders, some are sprouters and some are both. Seeders are often killed by fire, but the heat causes woody fruits of species like banksias, hakeas and casuarinas to open and release seeds. Other plants, such as acacias and peas, have already dropped seeds, many of which have been carried underground by ants where they are heated, but not burned. This heat is needed to split their hard coats, allowing moisture to penetrate and the seeds subsequently to germinate. They may remain viable in the ground for many decades, waiting for a fire, whereupon they are rewarded with a nutrient-rich ash bed, soil sterilised of harmful bacteria and fungi, and a relative dearth of seed-eating predators. Curiously, experiments have shown that chemicals in smoke, rather than heat, are enough to stimulate germination in certain species.

Sprouters use two basic strategies. Many trees conceal a legion of dormant, epicormic buds beneath a thick layer of insulating bark. If the crown is destroyed, hormones awaken these buds, which rapidly shoot out sideways from the trunk, giving recovering trees a woolly, 'bottlebrush' appearance. Once the crown is re-established, new hormones suppress this growth and the shoots die off. Other trees, such as snow gums and mallee eucalypts, re-sprout from the base where lignotubers – massive, woody structures, with more repressed buds – have been insulated underground from the fire. These types of trees tend to be multi-stemmed and can survive for many hundreds of years in this way. Many eucalypts are sprouters, as are some grasses, sedges, banksias, hakeas and grevilleas.

WINNERS AND LOSERS

Studies have shown that biodiversity is often reduced in fire-prone habitats that are protected from fire for too long, but the relationship is a complex one. The intensity, frequency and season of the fire are all important: frequent fires may kill saplings before they have had a chance to produce seed but assist rapidly regenerating plants; adaptable sprouters may be killed by too many intense fires; other plants may become extinct if they have to wait too long or the fire was not intense enough or came at the wrong time of year; and seeds germinating after spring fires may die off in summer heat or drought.

Epicormic shoots sprout from burnt trees. (SM)

Inevitably animals die in fires and many that flee the flames are killed by predators, but some employ effective survival strategies. Wombat burrows are excellent retreats and are often shared by lyrebirds, lizards and other small creatures. Damp places between rocks or under logs, and unburnt areas, also provide shelter, while koalas, gliders and possums may be safe in canopies or hollows if the flames are not too high or intense. Afterwards fresh, green shoots attract grazing mammals and herbivorous invertebrates – and their predators – with different species benefiting at different stages. Frequent fires favour some but not others, such as those needing dense cover. In general a mosaic of vegetation, burned at different times with different intensities, supports the greatest diversity of both plants and animals.

PEOPLE AND FIRE

Before humans arrived in Australia, lightning was the chief fire-starter. Charcoal records show a marked increase following the arrival of Aboriginal people, who used fire as a tool to make food more accessible. Europeans used it indiscriminately to clear vegetation but also feared it, trying to suppress blazes that threatened property and lives. As development increasingly encroaches on the forests today, substantial modern resources are devoted to control strategies. During risky periods total fire bans mean that not only campfires are prohibited but also use of machinery such as tractors, chainsaws and lawnmowers in case a spark might create an inferno. To reduce the risk of wildfires, controlled burns may be lit when weather is cool, humid and calm to reduce fuel loads, destroy weeds and to mimic natural conditions for conservation. Fire management is a complex and contentious issue, but it is generally agreed that a variety of fire regimes in any given habitat, varying in intensity and frequency, is most beneficial.

MAMMALS

The red kangaroo is the largest living marsupial. (FL/FLPA)

A ustralian mammals, like those throughout the world, grow fur – or hair – and produce milk for their young. Millions of years of isolation from other landmasses, however, has resulted in the evolution of some unique, even downright eccentric, characteristics. Since European settlement, 379 species have been recorded from Australia. Of these, 357 are native (though some have since become extinct). They comprise two monotremes, 159 marsupials, 76 bats, 64 rodents and one placental land carnivore (dingo), as well as ten seals, 44 cetaceans and a single sirenian. The remaining 22 species have been introduced.

MONOTREMES

Monotremes – the platypus and echidnas – are found only in Australia and New Guinea. These extraordinary creatures combine features of both mammals and reptiles. Like all mammals, they are warm-blooded, grow fur and produce milk – although this milk seeps from mammary glands rather than being delivered via nipples. Like reptiles, they lay eggs and have just one ventral opening – a cloaca – that is used both for reproduction and passing waste; the term 'monotreme' means 'with one hole'.

Monotreme eggs have a leathery shell, like those of snakes or turtles. The platypus mother holds her eggs (usually two or three) between her curled-up tail and her belly, while the echidna rolls her single egg into a muscular pouch on her belly. The baby monotreme hatches after about ten days. Known as a puggle, it is poorly developed but grows fast.

PLATYPUS

When, in 1798, the skin of a platypus (*Ornithorhynchus anatinus*) was first sent to England, it was regarded as a hoax. The British Museum's George Shaw, believing a duck's beak and feet had been attached to the head of a mammal, attempted to unpick the stitches with scissors. It would take another 100 years before Europeans believed Australian claims that the platypus lays eggs.

Underwater, a platypus uses its bill to smell and taste, and to detect electrical impulses. (FNS/FLPA)

This bizarre animal is 40–60cm long and dark brown, with a rounded tail and duck-like bill. It lives in freshwater rivers, streams, dams and lakes throughout eastern Australia, including Tasmania. With a normal body temperature of 32°C, compared with 37–38°C for most mammals, and fur that is denser than even that of river otters and polar bears, it is able to survive in almost freezing water, as well as in the tropics. Tasmanian platypuses weigh twice as much (2kg) as those living in north Queensland. The male has two hollow, curved spurs, connected to poison glands, just above the heel of each hind leg. These are probably used in disputes between rivals during the mating season, from July to October. The venom is strong enough to cause severe pain in humans.

The platypus is generally most active between dusk and dawn, diving to feed on insects, crustaceans, worms, small fishes and frogs. Closing its eyes, ears and nostrils underwater, it uses its sensitive bill to search for prey. This bill is not hard, like a duck's, but soft and rubbery. It contains electro-sensors, which are not only sensitive to touch but can also detect the slight electrical impulses generated by muscle movements of prey. The platypus stores food in its cheeks until it surfaces to breathe, when it grinds its catch between hard pads in the upper and lower jaw. Although it usually surfaces frequently, this animal can stay underwater for up to 14 minutes because its blood is rich in oxygen-carrying haemoglobin, and it is able to reduce its oxygen requirements by lowering its heart rate from over 200 beats per minute to fewer than ten.

Out of the water, a platypus conceals itself in a burrow with a small entrance at, or just below, the water line. It may have several 1–3m-long 'camping' burrows, used for rest or refuge, but the nursery burrow is up to 30m long. Before giving birth, the mother walls herself in to keep out snakes, goannas and water rats. Later, when leaving to feed, she plugs the entrance with soil.

SPOTTING A PLATYPUS

Platypuses are surprisingly common, despite the threats posed by habitat destruction, discarded fishing paraphernalia, litter, pollution and pumping machinery. Quiet waterways are the best places to see them, generally at dusk and dawn and sometimes during overcast days.

Platypuses swim on the surface between dives. (AF/FLPA)

The secret to platypus spotting is patience. Ask local people for tips on hotspots and watch quietly for the telltale bow-wave of a swimming platypus, or the splash and circular ripple pattern it makes when diving. These animals tend to surface every couple of minutes, usually within 25m of their last appearance, so if you have just glimpsed one, simply keep scanning the water surface. Water rats (see page 65) can be mistaken for platypuses in the water, but have visible ears and long tails. Turtles can also raise false hopes.

Echidnas are active both by day and by night. (GW)

The long fur of Tasmanian echidnas almost hides their spines. (DW)

SHORT-BEAKED ECHIDNA

The short-beaked echidna (*Tachyglossus aculeatus*) is found in Australia and New Guinea, with the latter also being home to three species of long-beaked echidna. Quite abundant in some locations, it is the only native mammal to inhabit every part of the country, including deserts, humid tropics and freezing alpine heights.

An echidna is about the size of a rabbit. It is covered with brown, white-tipped spines, which grow through a coat of dark, softer fur; in Tasmanian echidnas this fur is almost long enough to conceal the spines. A foraging individual wanders along with a slow, rolling gait, rather like that of a monitor lizard. If threatened, it wedges itself under a log or rock with just its spines visible, or digs rapidly into soft ground, disappearing like a sinking ship. On hard surfaces it may roll into a ball. Males have spurs on their hind feet, though these are not venomous.

In addition to its sensitive hearing and good sense of smell, an echidna detects prey using its long snout, which, like the platypus's bill, is equipped with electro-sensors. It feeds mainly on ants and termites, breaking into nests with its strong front feet and using its long, sticky tongue – measuring up to 18cm – to lap up the helpless occupants. The ability to flick its tongue in and out at a rate of 100 times per minute explains the scientific name, *Tachyglossus*, which means 'swift tongue'. In colder areas many echidnas become torpid in winter, lowering their body temperature from its normal 33°C to as low as 4°C, and breathing just once every three minutes to reduce their metabolic rate. They survive this period on stored body fat.

Echidnas are normally solitary. During the winter breeding season, however, up to a dozen males may form a train behind a female, following her for as long as six weeks until she is ready to mate. A series of head-pushing contests determines which suitor is successful, the winner digging in beside the female for a mating session that can last a few hours. The female initially carries the baby in her pouch after the egg hatches. At about two months, however, it becomes too heavy and prickly, so she hides it in a burrow, feeding it only every 5–10 days. The youngster is independent at about seven months old.

MARSUPIALS

Marsupials are mammals with pouches. Although this arrangement was once regarded as primitive, many human mothers consider it an evolutionary upgrade, as the infant is born while still a tiny embryo. Blind, hairless, and looking rather like a jellybean – except for its quite well-developed front legs – the newborn hauls itself up through its mother's belly hair to reach her pouch, a journey that takes just a few minutes. On arrival, it attaches itself to a teat – the end of which swells inside its mouth, locking it in place – and the maturing process continues. When it has grown fur and is able to maintain its own body temperature, the youngster ventures out of the pouch on forays, returning to feed and to escape danger. Males too have distinctive reproductive features: the scrotum of all marsupial males hangs in front of the penis, which, in most cases, has a bifurcated end (females have a double vagina). A male is able at will – when fighting, for example – to retract its scrotum completely inside its body. Although iconically Australian, one-third of all marsupials are found in South America, with an additional 60 or more species in New Guinea and a few in Indonesia. Australia has about 160 species, varying in size from tiny 4-gram planigales to male red kangaroos weighing up to 90kg.

KOALA

The koala (*Phascolarctos cinereus*) is an extremely laid-back creature. Deriving little spare energy from its diet of nutrient-poor eucalypt leaves, which take 200 hours to digest, it spends about 20 hours a day asleep or resting. Even its brain is an energy saver, being so small that it does not even fill the skull; presumably better-fed ancestors were brainier.

A koala joey stays with its mother for about 12 months. (GE/FLPA)

There is just one species of koala, which stands alone in its own genus and family and is certainly not a bear. It is found on the eastern mainland, from north Queensland to Victoria and in coastal South Australia. Koalas in the north are grey-brown, but those in the south are dark brown and have thicker fur and longer ear tufts. Northern animals are also smaller: males average 70.5cm long and weigh 6.5kg, while southern males are, on average, 78cm and 12kg. Females are 2–4kg lighter than males. Rough pads, sharp claws and opposable digits (two on each front paw, one on each hind) allow the koala to climb well. On the hind foot two fused digits form a double claw for grooming. Curiously, koalas are the only animals other than humans that can boast individually unique fingerprints.

Adults are solitary, except at mating times, when amorous males grunt and bellow so loudly they may be heard a considerable distance away. This usually establishes dominance without conflict – a good idea, as combat between competing males can be violent. A month after mating, the female gives birth to a single offspring, which spends 6–7 months in the pouch. From about 22–30 weeks, as it begins to explore outside the pouch, the joey feeds on 'pap' – a specialised form of faeces thought to come from the mother's caecum. This mushy, protein-rich, first solid food allows it to acquire the micro-organisms necessary to digest gum leaves. As it grows, the youngster rides on its mother's back or abdomen, learning which leaves are palatable.

Although a koala eats only gum leaves (a couple of kilos per day), fewer than 10% of eucalypt species appear on its menu because it avoids those leaves with a high tannin or essential oil content. Unfortunately, the more nutritious leaves grow on soils that are also best for agriculture. In the past, more than three million koalas were killed for their skins, but habitat loss and bushfires are the species' main threats today. Dogs and vehicles are also a problem, killing more than 4,000 koalas each year, while widespread *Chlamydia* infection causes blindness and, in females, infertility.

When in koala territory, look out for them dozing in the upper parts of trees, either wedged in a fork or slumped on a horizontal branch. You might spot a white flash of chest fur or smell the pungent odour of a male on heat.

Wombats spend much of their time in burrows, snoozing or digging. (DH/FLPA)

WOMBATS

Wombats are thickset animals, with powerful limbs and broad, solid skulls that function as bulldozers. Among the world's largest burrowers, they create extensive, branching tunnel systems, up to 30m long and 5m deep, by digging with their front paws and then walking backwards to push the loose dirt out of the entrance. Their rumps have such thick skin, hair and bone that they can serve as shields to block the burrows, withstanding the bites of predators. These reinforced rear ends can even crush to death an intruding dingo, fox or

A female wombat produces a single offspring every two years. (AF/FLPA)

dog. Despite their solid build, wombats can maintain a speed of 40km/h over short distances, leap over metre-high fences and squeeze through amazingly small gaps.

Grass is the staple diet of wombats, though they may also dig up roots during dry times. They are extremely energy-efficient animals: a wombat feeds for just two–six hours a day, whereas an eastern grey kangaroo of the same weight has an 18-hour daily mealtime. Their very low metabolism has been described as almost reptilian and, like reptiles, wombats adjust their behaviour according to temperature. In winter they spend the cold nights in their burrows, coming out to feed in mornings or afternoons, but in summer emerge only at night. They also save energy by lowering their body temperature while they are sleeping.

Wombats are also among the most water-efficient mammals on earth and can survive droughts that kill other animals. They use only about 20% as much water as sheep and their droppings are four times drier than a camel's. Look out for these distinctive, cube-shaped deposits – often dropped in unlikely places, such as on top of rocks or clumps of prickly grasses.

A female wombat's pouch faces backwards so that her babies don't get earth kicked in their faces as she burrows. About a month after conception the newborn moves into the pouch for about a further ten months. As it matures, it sometimes pops out its head to nibble on grass – creating the impression that the mother has grown an extra head at her rear end. It then spends a further eight–ten months with mum after leaving the pouch. Wombats live, on average, for about 20 years.

There are three species of wombat. The common wombat (*Vombatus ursinus*) has dense, bristly, grey-brown fur, grows to about a metre in length and weighs up to 30kg, although those in Tasmania are about a third smaller. This species is common in Tasmania and the Australian Alps. Elsewhere, it is patchily distributed, in forest, coastal scrub and heath in southeast Australia, and in wet forests above 600m in northern New South Wales and southern Queensland. Southern and northern hairy-nosed wombats (*Lasiorhinus* spp) have softer fur, longer ears and square muzzles. The former has a fragmented distribution in semi-arid shrubland in central southern Australia. The latter (dubbed the 'uncommon wombat') is represented by fewer than 100 individuals inhabiting just 300ha of national park in inland Queensland. It is also the largest.

43

A mob of eastern grey kangaroos rests in shade during the heat of the day. (SM)

KANGAROOS, WALLABIES AND RELATIVES

Scientists believe that macropods (Macropodidae) evolved from a tree-dwelling, possum-like animal that descended to the ground. The musky rat-kangaroo, from Queensland's wet tropics, offers a clue to this evolutionary stage. Although it lives on the forest floor it has retained two key characteristics of the tree-climbers: a 'thumb-toe' – an opposable toe on its hind foot – and a prehensile tail. Most macropods, having lost these tree-climbing attributes, continued to adapt to life on the ground, their forms changing accordingly as forests shrank and grasslands spread. But one group – probably rock-wallabies, with their penchant for climbing – recognising a food source or a refuge from predators, headed back up into the canopy and became tree-kangaroos.

The name macropod means 'big footed', a reference to the large feet and powerful hind legs that give these animals their distinctive bounding gait. The muscles and tendons in these legs act like coiled springs, which stretch as the animal lands and recoil during take-off so that energy stored on landing from one hop is transferred to the next. Also, when it bounces up, a kangaroo's guts are pulled down, drawing air into the lungs and further saving energy normally used by chest muscles for breathing. Hopping is so energy-efficient in large macropods that studies, involving captive kangaroos on treadmills wearing oxygen masks, have shown that these animals actually expend less energy when moving faster and much less than they would if running. Interestingly, they would not have been able to evolve pelvises of sufficient strength for hopping if they did not give birth to such small, underdeveloped young. Four feet are more efficient for slow movement, so grazing macropods lean on their front legs to swing their back legs forward, using their large, strong tails for balance. On land most can only move their hind feet together but when swimming they kick their legs independently. Yes, roos can swim – usually to escape from predators, though one unfortunate individual seen entering the sea off a Victorian beach was killed by a shark.

Many adult female kangaroos and wallabies are almost permanently pregnant. Shortly after giving birth, with the little joey now in her pouch, mum mates and becomes pregnant again. However, development of this new embryo (a blastocyst) is put on hold and does not resume until the joey in the pouch has permanently left home – either when mature, after about 200 days, or if it dies. Production then recommences. A few weeks later a new joey is born and the pouch has a new resident. Mum mates again and soon a new blastocyst is stored, ready to be activated when required. This means mum has three babies: a joey at her side that will not be fully weaned for a few more months; a tiny joey attached to a teat in the pouch; and an embryo in her womb. Amazingly, she can supply two types of milk simultaneously: a fatty type for the older joey, which pops its head in for a drink from time to time, and a thin, carbohydrate-rich milk for the pouch young. Each youngster remains faithful to its own personal teat. These animals are thus perfectly adapted to Australian conditions. If stressed by drought, the female's milk may dry up and her suckling young die. The dormant blastocyst, however, is waiting in the wings. As soon as conditions improve, development begins. Populations recover quickly.

Although there were once carnivorous kangaroos, all today's macropods are herbivorous, existing very efficiently on a fairly poor diet of (often dry) grass and leaves.

SKIPPY ON THE PLATE?

Millions of kangaroos are legally culled each year, mainly because they compete with agriculture. Some conservationists argue that, since kangaroos are less destructive to the fragile environment than hoofed animals, adapt more naturally to drought and produce no climate-changing methane, they are a better source of food. Kangaroo meat is also low in saturated fat but high in healthy unsaturated omega-3 fatty acids, and slaughtering – a shot to the head in the wild – is more humane than in any abattoir. Kangaroo meat is available in supermarkets and increasing in popularity, especially with environmentally conscious carnivores.

Kangaroos

The male red kangaroo (*Macropus rufus*) is the body-builder of the kangaroo world: impressive but not especially pretty. The largest living marsupial, a male 'big red' weighs up to 90kg and can stretch to over 2m in height. It is also the supreme athlete, reaching 60km/h in short bursts, and covering 12m in the long jump and up to 3m in the high jump. Most males have rusty-coloured fur, while females, which weigh just half as much as males and sit up to about 1.2m, are generally a bluish grey and are

Except in central Australia, female red kangaroos are greyish. (AF/FLPA)

sometimes called 'blue fliers'. Both sexes have black and white, elongated patches on the sides of the muzzle. Red kangaroos hop with their bodies held almost horizontal to the ground and tails curving up. This species favours arid and semi-arid parts of Australia, where it is common and widespread. Large groups, known as mobs, gather on green growth after rain, resting in shade during the heat of the day.

The western grey kangaroo (left, IM) is browner, with a darker face, than the eastern grey (right, DW).

Grey kangaroos are a little smaller than red kangaroos – males weighing up to 70kg and standing up to about 1.6m – and hold themselves more upright when hopping. They also live in rather wetter areas, wherever the rainfall is over 250mm a year, forming mobs whose numbers fluctuate with conditions; a population increase due to land clearance has led to regular culling in some areas. There are two species. The eastern grey kangaroo (*M. giganteus*) is grey-brown with paler underparts. It lives in a variety of habitats, from farmland and woodland to semi-arid areas – and even alpine snow in eastern Australia. It is the only kangaroo in Tasmania, where it is known as the forester. The western grey (*M. fuliginosus*) is browner, with grey underparts and a black muzzle, and lives on the western mainland. The two species are found together where ranges overlap and can be approached quite closely in some public places.

The common wallaroo (*Macropus robustus*) sticks to rocky hills, where it can shelter from the heat of the day in caves and under ledges. It is a stocky kangaroo with quite an upright stance. Individuals in the east of its range tend to be darker, sometimes almost black, with thick, shaggy fur, while those in more arid parts, where they are known as euros, have shorter fur that ranges from brown or grey-brown to orange-red. Males weigh up to 55kg, stand to 1.6m and are always darker in colour than the much smaller females. The antilopine wallaroo (*M. antilopinus*), from monsoonal eucalypt woodlands across northern Australia, is less stocky and shaggy than the common wallaroo. Males are reddish tan – and can be mistaken for red kangaroos – while females have greyish shoulders.

Large numbers of agile wallabies graze in grassy areas of the northern tropics. (GW)

Wallabies

Wallabies differ from kangaroos only in minor ways. Most noticeably, wallabies are smaller, adults weighing no more than 30kg. They also have slightly different molars and the length of the leg between ankle and knee is proportionally shorter – generally frequenting less open terrain, wallabies do not have the same need for speed. As with kangaroos, male wallabies are taller and more muscular than females, and usually weigh at least twice as much.

The agile wallaby (*Macropus agilis*) is the most common wallaby in tropical coastal plains, where it inhabits grassy open forests and riverine floodplains, as well as grassy suburban areas. It is sandy brown, with contrasting white and black stripes on the sides of the muzzle and a pale hip stripe. Males weigh up to 27kg and sit up to 1.2m. Groups spend the day in the shelter of trees, emerging in the late afternoon, or earlier on overcast days, to graze.

The whiptail wallaby (*M. parryi*) is a slender wallaby with a very long tail. It is pale grey-brown and has a distinctive dark brown face with contrasting white stripes running along each side of the muzzle – hence its common name of 'pretty-faced wallaby'. The outer sides of its ears are also adorned with white stripes, bordered by dark fur. Males weigh up to 26kg and sit up to 1.2m. These wallabies form mobs of up to 50 animals in grassy open forests in the coastal areas of Queensland and northern New South Wales.

The red-necked wallaby (*M. rufogriseus*), which is slightly smaller than the agile and whiptail

Red-necked wallabies are relatively solitary. (IM)

The black (swamp) wallaby prefers leafy shrubs to grasses. (DW)

wallabies, earns its name from the rusty-brown fur on the back of its neck and shoulders. Otherwise it is grey-brown. It is common in eucalypt forests and coastal scrub of the east and southeast. The Tasmanian form, known as Bennett's wallaby, is generally darker, shaggier and less obviously rufous – although a small population on Bruny Island is pure white.

The swamp or black wallaby (*Wallabia bicolour*) is considered to be the only surviving member of the separate genus *Wallabia*. It differs from *Macropus* wallabies in having fewer chromosomes and different teeth, while pregnant females mate before rather than after giving birth. Dark in colour and largely solitary, this macropod is common on the eastern mainland, where it browses on shrubs in forests and heathland rather than in swamps; black wallaby is the more accurate of its two names. It has a stocky build, a pale lower jaw, rufous around the ears and a hunched hopping posture. Males are slightly larger than females, weighing up to 20kg and sitting up to about 70cm high.

Red-necked pademelons seldom venture far from the forest edge. (IM)

Pademelons are medium-sized wallabies that weigh 4–9kg. They spend their days under forest or scrub cover, browsing on fallen leaves and fruits, but at dusk move out into surrounding open areas to feed on grass until dawn. Their fur is grey-brown, with areas of rich rufous that vary in position between species. The red-legged pademelon (*Thylogale stigmatica*) is common in northern rainforests, although the warning thump of a startled animal taking off is often the only indication of its presence. This species overlaps with the red-necked pademelon (*T. thetis*) in the forests of southeast Queensland and northeast New South Wales. The rufous-bellied pademelon (*T. billardierii*) is now confined to Tasmania, where it is very common.

The quokka (*Setonix brachyurus*) is a stocky little wallaby, weighing not much more than 4kg. It has brown fur and a relatively short tail. Though now very rare on the mainland, good numbers thrive on fox-free islands, notably Rottnest Island, near Perth.

Early Dutch explorers thought quokkas were rats. (IM)

Black-footed rock-wallabies have a scattered distribution in the arid zone. (GW)

Rock-wallabies

There are at least 15 species of rock-wallaby (*Petrogale* spp), most restricted to relatively small ranges. Adults weigh 1–11kg, depending on species, and can sit up to 60cm in height. As their name suggests, these wallabies live in rocky regions, sheltering by day in caves and crevices, and feeding at night on grasses and leaves from trees and shrubs. They are very sure-footed, bounding effortlessly up steep inclines and sloping tree trunks on the granulated, gripping soles of their relatively short feet.

Rock-wallabies usually live in colonies, some with as many as 100 members. They usually hide away by day in hot weather but can be seen sunning themselves in late afternoons and early mornings, sometimes appearing during the day in winter. It is always worthwhile scrutinising a rocky area carefully: these animals are well camouflaged but once you see one, you may notice others. Competition with feral goats is reducing populations in some places, while foxes and cats sometimes prey on them, as do traditional foes such as dingoes, pythons and eagles. Some species face extinction. In eastern Queensland, nine different species, seven of which appear identical in the field, inhabit separate ranges between Cape York Peninsula and the New South Wales border. The black-footed rock-wallaby (*P. lateralis*) is quite common in rocky gorges in arid areas.

Tree-kangaroos

In the rainforests of north Queensland, kangaroos live in trees. In fact, ten different species pursue this odd lifestyle: two in Australia and eight more in New Guinea. Tree-kangaroos are adept climbers, although they never re-evolved the prehensile tail and the opposable toe of their possum ancestors. Like possums (and unlike terrestrial kangaroos) they can move their legs independently and walk, as well as hop, using their long heavy tails for balance. Compared with other kangaroos, they have stronger forelimbs, relatively short but broad hind feet, long curved claws, and wrists and ankles that allow their feet to twist and grasp branches. When descending, a tree-kangaroo walks or slides down the trunk backwards, rather like a human. Individuals have been recorded jumping to the ground

Lumholtz's tree-kangaroos, mother and joey. (DW)

from heights of 20m, apparently without harm – although autopsies have found old breaks in the bones of many.

Tree-kangaroos are mainly nocturnal but do move about by day. They eat leaves and some fruit – a low-energy diet that fuels a low-activity lifestyle. With their solitary habits, restricted distributions, low numbers and concealment among tall trees, tree-kangaroos are not often seen. They sometimes come down to the ground to raid crops (they like pumpkins) and to cross from one tree – or forest patch – to another. Unfortunately this brings them into often fatal contact with dogs and vehicles, a fate that is becoming more common as their habitat is cleared and fragmented.

Lumholtz's tree-kangaroo (*Dendrolagus lumholtzi*) is the smallest 'tree-roo' species, weighing about 6–9kg. Its body is about 60cm long, with an even longer tail. Its dark face contrasts with an encircling, pale cream headband, and its dark grey-brown back with a pale belly and black feet. Although once found in the lowlands, before most of the forest was cleared, today it survives in the higher forests of the Atherton Tableland area. It prefers forest edges and is easier to see than the much bigger (14kg) Bennett's tree-kangaroo (*D. bennettianus*), which lives between the Daintree River and Cooktown.

BETTONGS AND POTOROOS

These animals look like small wallabies but belong to the Potoroidae family and differ from macropods in their teeth, stomachs and limb proportions. They also have weakly prehensile tails, a link to their possum ancestors. Two members of the family have become extinct since European settlement and many others are endangered due to habitat loss and the introduction of foxes and rabbits. This is unfortunate, as most species play an important role in maintaining forest ecosystems by eating truffles (see page 30). The rufous bettong (*Aepyprymnus rufescens*) is

Rufous bettongs use strong claws to dig for tubers and truffles. (T&PG/FLPA)

the largest and best-known member of the family. Grey-brown with a rufous tinge and weighing up to 3.5kg, it inhabits grassy woodlands from northern Queensland to northern New South Wales, sometimes hopping about campgrounds at night. Potoroos are stockier, with darker fur and shorter ears and tails. The long-nosed potoroo (*Potorous tridactylus*) is no bigger than a rabbit. It is most common in eastern and northern Tasmania but is also found on the southeastern coastal mainland.

BANDICOOTS

Bandicoots (Peramelidae family) have coarse, brown fur and scamper around on all fours. Although sometimes mistaken for rats, they are actually native marsupials, with short tails and long, pointed muzzles that distinguish them from any rodent. Active at night, they use their strong, sharp-clawed forefeet to dig conical holes in search of worms and other invertebrates (to the annoyance of lawn-proud gardeners), and also forage for roots, seeds

Bandicoots sometimes bite off each other's tails in territorial encounters. (IM)

and berries. By day they shelter in nests of vegetation – or sometimes shallow scrapes – under dense cover.

Bandicoots have the shortest gestation period of any mammal: their two to four babies are born just 12.5 days after conception. As the youngsters make their way into the mother's backward-facing pouch they remain attached by an umbilical cord to a rudimentary placenta – a feature otherwise found only in koalas. Female bandicoots begin to reproduce when just four or five months old and do so every seven weeks if conditions are favourable. Despite this fecundity, two of the eight bandicoot species have become extinct since European settlement and the range of many others has shrunk considerably. The northern brown bandicoot (*Isoodon macrourus*), common in northern and eastern Australia, is the largest species, with males weighing up to 3kg. It frequents lowland suburban lawns and cane fields where, at harvest time, fleeing individuals often end up as roadkill.

The greater bilby (*Macrotis lagotis*) is very rarely seen outside captive breeding centres. This rabbit-sized marsupial has silky, blue-grey fur and enormously long ears. Formerly widespread, it is now restricted to a few remote desert areas. At night it digs holes to find invertebrates and tubers, sheltering by day in deep burrow systems. Bilbies breed rapidly, but predation by foxes, cats and dingoes, and competition from rabbits and cattle, have put them on the endangered list. Chocolate bilbies are sold as an Easter alternative to chocolate bunnies in order to highlight the plight of Australia's endangered native wildlife over that of this destructive import.

MUSKY RAT-KANGAROO

The musky rat-kangaroo (*Hypsiprymnodon moschatus*) is a singular little marsupial, in a family of its own, that combines features of both possums and macropods. Confined to the rainforests of north Queensland, it is about the size of a guinea-pig and has dark brown fur with a reddish tinge. You might come across this diurnal creature scuffling about in the leaf-litter, as it searches for fruits – many of them highly toxic to most other forest animals – seeds, fungi and invertebrates. Indeed, its habit of burying uneaten fruits and seeds makes it an important dispersal agent for rainforest trees. When making a nest, it coils its tail around bundles of twigs to carry them to the nook of a tree buttress or fallen log.

The musky rat-kangaroo can climb on low branches and rocks. (IM)

Common brushtails vary in colour. This coppery subspecies (*Johnstonii*) inhabits northeastern, upland rainforests. (IM)

POSSUMS AND GLIDERS

Possums are climbing marsupials not unlike nocturnal squirrels. They range in size but most are about as big as a small domestic cat. Larger, leaf-eating species are generally slow-moving while those that prefer nectar, tree sap, pollen, insects and other small animals tend to be quicker and more energetic. Many possums give birth to two or more young, which may ride around on the mother's back after they have left the pouch. Most species sleep in tree hollows.

Brushtail possums

The common brushtail possum (*Trichosurus vulpecula*), despite being nocturnal, is one of the most commonly seen native mammals. It has taken confidently to suburbia, often making its den in roof spaces and approaching people in caravan parks, campgrounds and so on. One of the largest possums, weighing up to 4kg, its fur is usually greyish above with a cream underside, but can vary from buff to dark and rufous. It has particularly large ears for a possum, and a furry tail with a hairless, friction strip on the underside to give it a better grip around branches. Feeding mainly on leaves and fruit – but willing to try almost anything – this possum lives wherever there are trees, especially those with hollows. In recent times, however, it has been mysteriously disappearing from drier areas of Australia. Brushtail possums have become a serious pest in New Zealand, where they were introduced for the fur trade. Over 70 million of them are now destroying forests and eating birds' eggs in ecosystems that evolved in the absence of mammals.

The mountain brushtail and short-eared possums (*T. cunninghamii* and *T. caninus*) live in wet sclerophyll and sub-tropical forests from central Queensland to Victoria. They are larger, stockier and darker than the common brushtail.

The green ringtail possum's low-energy diet includes many toxic leaves. (IM)

Ringtail possums

Ringtail possums have quite small, rounded ears, and can use their short-haired prehensile tails as a fifth limb when climbing. They are medium-sized possums, weighing about 1–2kg, and feed mainly on leaves – the choice varying with species. Some, if not all, recycle their food by eating their own droppings to extract extra nutrients. All are nocturnal.

The common ringtail possum (*Pseudocheirus peregrinus*) varies in colour from light and dark grey to brick red, with a pale underside, reddish patches on the limbs, white patches behind the ears and a white end to the tail. This species, which generally weighs less than 1kg, is common in the east and southeast mainland and in Tasmania, living in forests and woodlands where there is a dense shrub layer. It also frequents suburban gardens but, with a fondness for flowers and particularly rose buds, it is not always welcome. A social possum, it hangs out in family groups, communicating with soft chirps and twitters that are often mistaken for bird or insect calls. During the day family members snooze in tree hollows, or in round football-sized dreys made from twigs, bark and leaves carried in the curled tail.

Four ringtail possums are endemic to the upland rainforests of northeast Queensland. The most widely distributed, found down to about 300m, is the green ringtail (*Pseudochirops archeri*). It is not actually green, but a combination of black, silver and yellow fur gives it a mossy tinge that camouflages it well by day when it curls up on a branch to sleep. The adult Herbert River ringtail (*Pseudochirulus herbertensis*), from the southern wet tropics, is very dark brown with some white on the front – though the juvenile is fawn-coloured and looks like a small version of the Daintree River ringtail (*P. cinereus*), from further north. Both species are generally solitary, making nests in tree hollows or camping on epiphytes. The lemuroid possum (*Hemibelideus lemuroides*) has large eyes, which reminded Swedish zoologist Robert Collet of Madagascan lemurs, and can be distinguished from the other species by its bushier tail and snub nose. It is relatively energetic for a leaf-eating possum, leaping noisily between branches with legs spread like a glider – although it has only a rudimentary gliding membrane. This ringtail frequents altitudes above 450m. Most individuals are dark brown to grey, although a high proportion of the isolated population living above 1,100m on the Carbine Tablelands are creamy white.

Greater glider

Gliders are possums with flaps of skin on their sides, known as gliding membranes, that allow them to glide up to 100m between trees. The greater glider (*Petauroides volans*) is a large possum that belongs in the same family as the ringtail possums. It weighs up to 1.7kg, with a body about the size of a rabbit, a long (up to 60cm), bushy, non-prehensile tail and large furry ears. Colouration varies greatly from very pale grey to dark brown, but almost all those in the forests around Healesville, in Victoria, are pure white. This species is found along the east coast in tall eucalypt forests, particularly where there are large hollows for dens. Like the koala, it eats only eucalypt leaves and buds, and its large gut, necessary for the bacterial breakdown of tough leaves, may help explain its size.

Gliders save energy by 'flying' from tree to tree in their open forest habitats. (SL/FLPA)

Other gliders

Most other gliders belong to the Petauridae family. Their gliding membrane extends from wrist to ankle and all have long, lower incisors used to create, and maintain, wounds in the bark of eucalypt and acacia trees, from which sap, a staple food source, oozes. They also eat nectar, pollen, fruit and insects, a diet that provides them with more energy than the eucalypt-munching greater glider; the scientific name *Petaurus*, meaning 'rope-dancer', is a reference to their acrobatic lifestyle. Five species are superficially similar in appearance – light or olive grey, sometimes with a brownish tinge, pale underparts and a dorsal stripe of dark grey fur from the forehead to lower back. It has been suggested that this could look like a strip of sap to an owl and thus serve to camouflage feeding gliders from these nocturnal predators.

The sugar glider (*P. breviceps*) is found around the northern, eastern and southeastern margins of the mainland, as well as in Tasmania, where it may have been introduced. It is common in many areas of wet and dry sclerophyll woodland, especially where old-growth trees provide nesting hollows. This is a small possum, weighing less than 150g, with a maximum total body and tail length of 400mm. It is also very sociable for a possum: up to seven adults and their young may share a den, snuggling together in a torpid state during cold weather and making an intimidating chattering sound when disturbed. Dominant males use scent glands to mark territory and other group members; they can be aggressive to any animal that doesn't smell quite right.

The squirrel glider (*P. norfolcensis*) is larger and heavier than the sugar glider. It lives in dry sclerophyll forests along the east coast, from north Queensland to Victoria. Larger still, the yellow-bellied glider (*P. australis*) is the biggest member of this group, weighing up to 700g with a maximum body and tail length of 800mm. It lives in wet sclerophyll forests in north Queensland and, patchily, along the east coast from central Queensland to mid-

The striped possum's bold stripes may confuse predatory owls. (GW)

Victoria. The underparts of older animals can be bright yellow – though not in northeast Queensland, where they are known as fluffy gliders for their long bushy tails. Favourite sap trees become quite heavily scarred and attract other possums, insects and birds.

The striped possum (*Dactylopsila trivirgata*) belongs to the Petauridae family but is not a glider. This slender, guinea-pig-sized possum weighs up to 500g and measures about 600mm in total length. Sporting a distinctive black and white striped coat and a white Y marking on the face, it lives in rainforest and open woodland, at most altitudes, in parts of northeast Queensland (as well as in New Guinea and beyond). This energetic possum has the largest brain, relative to body size, of any marsupial. It feeds largely on invertebrates, particularly beetle larvae, tapping on rotten wood to detect cavities and listening for movement. It then rips into the wood with powerful, lower incisors and inserts its elongated fourth (ring) finger to winkle out the unfortunate grub. It also eats flowers, pollen, native bee honey and fruit. The distinctive, sweet, musky smell of these possums, along with the sound of shaken branches and falling debris, helps to locate them.

Small possums

A number of very active, mouse-sized possums are found around Australia but, being small and nocturnal, are rarely seen. They feed largely on nectar and pollen, and are important pollinators, though they also eat invertebrates and even small skinks. Sadly, small possums are sometimes mistaken for mice and are trapped or poisoned. There are five species of pygmy possum. Four are mainly tree-dwellers but the mountain pygmy possum (*Burramys parvus*) lives among rocks at above 1,400m in the Australian Alps; its tiny home range is threatened by habitat loss and global warming.

The feathertail glider (*Acrobates pygmaeus*) is the only Australian member of the family Acrobatidae. Weighing little more than 10g, with a maximum total body and tail length of 160mm, it is the smallest gliding mammal in the world and has been known to cover 28m in a single glide. A high-energy diet of nectar, small insects and tree sap fuels a hyperactive lifestyle and this animal's scientific name, 'little acrobat' is very apt. Grey above and white below, it has a distinctive feather-like tail with long stiff hairs on either side that acts as a rudder during glides and can grip small branches. It also has an amazing ability to cling to almost any surface – even vertical glass – thanks to the minute ridges and sweat glands on its feet that create tiny, sticky strips. This glider lives in wet eucalypt forests around the eastern and southeastern mainland. It prefers diverse, mature forests with year-round flowering and tree hollows for nests. Up to 20 may share one nest; snuggling together for warmth they can enter a state of torpor for several days in winter as their body temperature drops as low as 2°C. The female produces up to four young, each of which is smaller than a grain of rice when it moves into the pouch. Like kangaroos, the female feathertail mates soon after giving birth, the new embryos remaining in a state of suspended development until those from the previous litter have ceased suckling.

The honey possum (*Tarsipes rostratus*) is the only member of the Tarsipedidae family. Strictly speaking this animal is not a possum and does not eat honey! Mouse-coloured, it has three dark stripes along its back and a long snout with a brush-tipped tongue for feeding on nectar and pollen; its foraging behaviour has been described as a cross between that of a monkey and a honeybee. The honey possum is locally common in the heathlands of Western Australia, where a rich abundance of flowers ensures a perpetual supply of food – banksias being favourites. Averaging about 10g in weight, it is one of the smallest marsupials. Males, however, sport the largest testes relative to body size of any mammal (4.2%) and produce the world's longest mammalian sperm (0.36mm). Females are about one-third larger and give birth to the world's smallest mammal baby, weighing just 0.0005g.

CARNIVOROUS MARSUPIALS (DASYURIDS)

Australia does not have any big cats or other carnivores that might be considered dangerous to humans. Pound for pound, however, the carnivorous marsupials of the order Dasyuromorphia are about as ferocious as a predator can get; most of them just happen to be quite small. The extinct thylacine, or Tasmanian tiger, weighing about 35kg, was the largest at the time of European settlement, but the last thylacine died in Hobart zoo in 1936. Apart from the numbat, all extant marsupial carnivores are in the Dasyuridae, or 'hairy-tailed', family. Most do not have permanent pouches. Instead, as a female becomes sexually active, folds of skin, or a fleshy rim, develop around her mammary glands. She gives birth to as many as 30 very tiny young but only the first ones to reach a nipple survive; she can further limit her litter by stopping the flow of milk to one or more teats.

The young must hold firm to the nipples, where they dangle like bunches of grapes as they grow. Living fast, dasyurids generally die young, many males lasting just one year and females only two or three. This reduces competition for food when the young mature.

Tasmanian devils use powerful jaws and teeth to crunch through bones. (CB/FLPA)

Tasmanian devil

Largest of the dasyurids, the Tasmanian devil (*Sarcophilus harrisi*) weighs up to 9kg and is about the size of a small, stocky dog. Its fur is black with white patches, usually on the chest. It has a large head with pink skin showing around the muzzle and eyes, and strong jaws. Hunting at night, this powerful predator kills anything up to the size of a small wallaby, and also feeds on roadkill or carrion washed up on beaches. Several may gather in squabbling groups around a carcass, uttering the ferocious snarls and screeches that are responsible for their unflattering name.

Although devils disappeared from the mainland about 5,000 years ago, following the introduction of the dingo, until recently they were common and widespread in Tasmania. However, a virulent, contagious, facial cancer that is passed between the animals – mainly through biting, particularly when mating – has in recent years devastated the population to the point where the species is now endangered. Attempts are being made to quarantine healthy populations.

The spotted-tailed quoll is the only Australian mammal with spots on its tail. (GW)

Quolls

These largely nocturnal hunters have a feisty temperament and can be quite aggressive if cornered. Though sometimes called native cats, they more closely resemble weasels or polecats. Four species live in Australia. All have fawn, brown or black fur with distinctive white spots on their bodies, long tails, pointed muzzles and sharp teeth used to kill prey with a bite to the back of the neck. Food varies with size of quoll, ranging from invertebrates, frogs, birds and eggs to possums and even wallabies. These predators were common and much more widespread before European settlement, but were subsequently persecuted due to their liking for poultry. They have also suffered from a disease epidemic (probably spread by cats), fox introductions, habitat loss and the spread of cane toads –

numbers crash when this poisonous, introduced amphibian moves into their territories. Most now inhabit just a fraction of their former range.

The eastern quoll (*Dasyurus viverrinus*) disappeared from the mainland following the spread of foxes but is common in Tasmania, where both fawn and black forms can be seen. Weighing less than 1kg, it hunts on the ground. The much larger (4–7kg) spotted-tailed quoll (*D. maculatus*) is an excellent climber and often targets prey in the canopy. It is reasonably secure in Tasmania but sparsely distributed elsewhere in its range on the southeast mainland and in north Queensland.

Antechinuses

Antechinuses look rather like small rats or large mice but have much more pointed noses and are ferocious carnivores, feeding on invertebrates and small lizards. They are mainly nocturnal but are sometimes out and about during the day, particularly during the winter mating season. Highly active, they race across the ground and into trees with fast, jerky movements. For males, the fortnight-long mating season is a fatal frenzy. They run around, day and night, mating as often and for as long as possible, their love-making sessions lasting for 5–12 hours. The female has little choice in the matter since she is held captive throughout by the scruff of the neck. At the end of the season the exhausted males have lost about 40% of their body weight and, overwhelmed with stress hormones and a breakdown of their immune systems, soon die. A month later their widows give birth to up to 12 young.

The yellow-footed antechinus (*Antechinus flavipes*) is widespread in mainland forests and heathlands and sometimes seen in suburban gardens and houses. Its grey head contrasts with

Antechinuses are excellent climbers. (CM/FLPA)

yellowish or reddish body fur and it has pale eye-rings. This species is the most likely to be out and about during the day – either on the ground or in trees. It is very agile and can even run along the underside of branches.

Other dasyurids

Other dasyurids are generally small to tiny – most weigh little more than a small coin – but are ferocious out of all proportion to their size. With sharply pointed teeth they attack mainly invertebrates but may also target small birds, lizards and mammals. Being nocturnal, they are rarely seen. The 19 species of dunnart (*Sminthopsis* spp) occur in almost every habitat, those in deserts obtaining their water from their prey and adapting their breeding according to rainfall. Some store energy, as fat, in their tails. Dunnarts are small and mouse-like with large eyes and ears and a ferocious temperament. If cornered they face the threat with a defiant, open-mouthed posture, while making faint hissing noises. Planigales (*Planigale* spp) are tiny and have particularly flat skulls, this feature allowing them to wriggle into rock crevices and cracks in dried mud in search of invertebrate prey. The two phascogales (*Phascogale* spp) are somewhat larger. Their tails end in a distinctive bottlebrush of dark hairs that can spring erect if the animal is alarmed or excited; possibly this serves to direct the attention of predators away from the body and head. They are acrobatic climbers.

NUMBAT

The numbat (*Myrmecobius fasciatus*) is diurnal because it eats only termites, which are most active when the soil is warm (though they retreat from the heat in the middle of a summer's day). It was once widespread across much of arid and semi-arid southern Australia but, thanks to habitat loss, introduced predators and altered burning patterns, is now restricted to small remnant patches of wandoo and jarrah forest in Western Australia. A numbat is the size of a small cat, with a long bushy tail and very pointed muzzle. Its fur is red on the shoulders and black on the rear, with several prominent white bars across the back. It often shelters in hollow logs, and feeds on the ground by breaking open termite nests with strong claws in order to lick up termites with its very long, sticky tongue.

The unusual numbat is the only member of the family Myrmecobiidae. (MW/FLPA)

Spectacled flying-foxes are vital dispersers of rainforest plant seeds in north Queensland. (IM)

PLACENTAL MAMMALS

Placental mammals – and that includes us – give birth to relatively well-developed young that have been nourished by the mother's blood, in the womb, via a placenta. Australia has about 195 native placental mammal species, 140 of them terrestrial and 55 marine (see page 153). Most arrived only after Australia collided with the Asian plate, about 15 million years ago.

BATS

Bats are the only mammals capable of true flight. The name of the order, Chiroptera, means 'hand-wing' and reflects the way in which the wings are supported on bones similar to those in our arms, with a thin, tough wing membrane stretched over greatly elongated 'finger' bones. About 80 bat species, roughly half of them endemic, are found in Australia, the majority in the warmer, northern parts. They belong to two quite distinct sub-orders: the megachiroptera (fruit bats and flying-foxes) and the microchiroptera. The micros eat mainly insects and most rely on sonar (echolocation) to navigate. They seek out dark places to roost and can hibernate. Megas, by contrast, eat nectar, pollen and fruit, and they use their eyes and good sense of smell to move about and find food. Most roost in open places and they do not hibernate. There are also many anatomical differences between the two sub-orders and it is possible they are not related at all but represent different – though strongly convergent – evolutionary lines. Indeed, it has even been suggested, controversially, that megabats are related to primates.

Flying-foxes heading out to feed at dusk are an impressive spectacle. (NB/FLPA)

Fruit bats and flying-foxes

The megabat group includes some very small blossom bats and rather bizarre, tube-nosed bats but, being relatively solitary, these are not often seen. Flying-foxes, on the other hand, roost in large, noisy, squabbling, treetop camps, sometimes in urban areas, streaming out by the thousand at dusk. Weighing up to 1kg, with wingspans of up to 1m, they have dog- or fox-like faces, large eyes and complex social and communication systems. Pollen and nectar are staple foods and these bats – flying up to 50km each night – are important pollinators for many trees, which produce pale flowers and increase nectar flow after dark to encourage their visits. They are also fruit-eaters, usefully distributing seeds as they fly over open areas, although this diet creates conflict with fruit farmers. Flying-foxes sometimes skim over water, including the sea, to soak their fur with water for drinking – though in tropical areas this brings the risk of being snapped up by leaping crocodiles.

The little red flying-fox (*Pteropus scapulatus*) has reddish-brown fur and relatively translucent wings when seen in flight. Responding nomadically to flowering, it is the most widespread species, found along the coast and quite far inland. Huge numbers – a million or more – can form temporary camps, especially during the October–November mating season. The grey-headed flying-fox (*P. poliocephalus*) is the largest Australian bat. It has dark fur, with an orange-red collar, and lives along the east coast from southern Queensland to Victoria. The black flying-fox (*P. alecto*) prefers mangrove and paperbark swamps around the tropical coast, south to northern New South Wales. The spectacled flying-fox (*P. conspicillatus*) has pale eye-rings and a blond nape that contrasts with its otherwise black fur. It inhabits rainforests in northeast Queensland, plus nearby open forests and orchards.

Insectivorous bats

Microbats can often be seen flittering about at dusk. They are superb aerialists, using hairs on the surface of their thin wings to sense air flow. These bats are particularly common in the tropics; those further south migrate or enter a state of torpor from about April to September. Identifying species is difficult. Most live in forests and many social species form massive roosting colonies in caves, roofs and other dark places, flowing out at dusk in a steady stream. Insectivorous bats are not blind but their eyes are generally small. Most rely on echolocation, building up a detailed sonic 'picture' of their surroundings and prey movements from the returning echoes of high-pitched sounds they emit. Nose-sonar (leaf-nosed) bats have bizarre faces with flaps of skin around their nostrils to channel sound into their noses for analysis. Mouth-sonar bats lack these ornaments and fly with their mouths open to collect their echoes. Microbats catch huge numbers of insects, eating up to half their body weight in one night. Some are very sensitive to disturbance and may abandon their young, so please consider this when exploring their caves. Sitting near a cave entrance at dusk to watch them emerge is more bat-friendly.

The ghost bat (*Macroderma gigas*), with a body the size of a small rat and a 1m wingspan, is one of the world's largest microbats. It supplements an insect diet with frogs, lizards, birds and small mammals, and – having only weak sonar – relies upon good eyesight and hearing to detect prey, killing it swiftly with strong bites. The name comes from its pale colour and thin, ghostly wings. Ghost bats live in both arid and rainforested areas across northern Australia, but numbers are declining – particularly as caves, vital for maternity camps, are destroyed by mining.

Diadem leaf-nosed bat (*Hipposideros diadema*). (GW)

The lesser long-eared bat (*Nyctophilus geoffroyi*) inhabits all regions except for northern and northeastern Queensland. It flies around streetlights at night and roosts almost anywhere, including blinds, gaps in timber and even clothes left hanging. This adaptability may be the secret to its success. The eastern horseshoe bat (*Rhinolophus megaphyllus*) is locally common along the east coast, particularly in Queensland. It has an elaborate nose-leaf and enormous ears. The northern freetail – or mastiff – bat (*Chaerephon jobensis*) is common throughout the tropics, where it sometimes forms colonies in roof spaces. Stray individuals, possibly babies or adults confused by extremely hot or wet conditions, occasionally turn up inside houses. The similar white-striped freetail bat (*Tadarida australis*) lives in the southern two-thirds of the continent.

Bentwing bats, named for their unusual fingers, are found across the tropical north and east coast, where they form massive maternity colonies in summer. About 80% of the known Australian population of little bentwings (*Miniopterus australis*) can be visited at Mount Etna Caves National Park in Queensland. The large-footed myotis (*Myotis* spp) specialises in raking its large feet across water to capture aquatic insects and small fish.

Sometimes called false vampire bats, ghost bats have carnivorous appetites. (DH/FLPA)

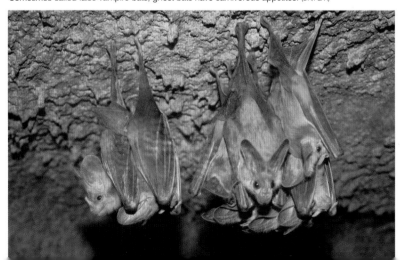

Melomyses feed on plant material, climbing with the aid of semi-prehensile tails. (GW)

RATS AND MICE

All Australian rodents belong to just one of the world's 24 rodent families, Muridae, and to just two of its 16 subfamilies. This lack of diversity probably reflects their relatively recent arrival (see page 8). Nonetheless, rodents represent about 25% of Australia's native mammal species. The first arrivals, the 'old endemics' (Hydromyinae) are the most diverse, with over 50 species. They are known as mosaic-tailed rats because the scales on their tails are arranged in an interlocking pattern. Melomyses look like large mice and are sometimes found scurrying around houses. The grassland melomys (*Melomys burtoni*) is the most widespread, living along the eastern and northern mainland coastal areas in open woodland and grasslands. Campers in north Queensland may become more familiar than they would like with the giant white-tailed rat (*Uromys caudimaculatus*). Weighing up to 1kg, this species has a pure white end to its tail, as if dipped in paint, and a formidable bite. It chews noisily into the hardest of nuts, including coconuts, as well as mud crabs, cupboards, backpacks and canned food – rainforest residents are convinced it can read labels, as it shows a preference for baked beans, condensed milk and beer; one individual has even been observed unscrewing the lid of a jam jar. And don't think your food will be safe in a tree: these rats are expert climbers.

Hopping-mice, which live mostly in arid sandy areas, have big ears and bound around on large back feet. Gregarious, they shelter in burrow systems by day and after rains populations can increase rapidly. The spinifex hopping-mouse (*Notomys alexis*) of central and western Australia can sometimes be seen in large numbers in Uluru campgrounds. Pebble-mound mice (*Pseudomys* spp), which inhabit mainly arid areas, collect small stones around their burrow entrances, sometimes covering an area of several metres. These pebbles may protect and insulate the burrows, collect dew and/or be infused with scent information.

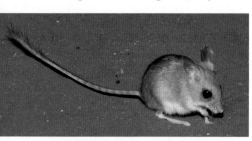

Desert-dwelling spinifex hopping-mice derive moisture from vegetation and insects. (MW/FLPA)

Australia's largest rodent, the water rat (*Hydromys chrysogaster*), is found widely in both fresh- and saltwater habitats. Behaving rather like an otter, it is the only semi-aquatic mammal in Australia besides the platypus. You might confuse the two when they are diving and surfacing, but the water rat has a long, furry tail with a white tip (it is not one of the mosaic-tailed group) and no bill. It also tends to leave the water to eat prey, scampering along the riverbank to a favourite feeding area marked with a midden of inedible parts. Water rats eat a variety of invertebrates and small vertebrates, including cane toads, which they have learned to flip over in order to avoid the poisonous shoulder glands.

Tail scales on the 'new endemic', or 'true' rats (Murinae) are arranged in overlapping rings with visible hairs. Members of this group, including introduced species (see page 66), can reproduce rapidly and favourable conditions, particularly rain in arid areas, can stimulate a sudden population explosion. Because of this, the long-haired rat (*Rattus villosissimus*) is also known as the plague rat. A boom

Water rats may feed on carrion, such as this dead black swan. (T&PG/FLPA)

in its numbers leads, in turn, to an irruption of raptors and other predators, followed by an equally dramatic bust. The native dusky rat (*R. colletti*), lives in dense numbers in the floodplains of northwest Northern Territory, attracting huge numbers of water pythons.

DINGO

The dingo (*Canis lupus dingo*), the only placental carnivore considered a native, hitched a lift from Asia with seafaring humans about 4,000 years ago and spread through much of the mainland. It is a primitive, medium-sized dog that howls but doesn't bark. Most dingoes are sandy red, although some are pale or dark. Cross-breeding with domestic dogs is common, and pure-bred individuals are now rare. Dingoes sometimes hunt alone and sometimes in packs, the latter allowing them to target large prey. The demise of the thylacine and the Tasmanian devil on the mainland is attributed to the dingo, which didn't reach Tasmania. Most dingoes are shy and wary of people, but on Queensland's Fraser Island feeding by locals and tourists has led to overconfident animals attacking people.

The dingo was domesticated in Asia before going wild in Australia. (SY/FLPA)

Feral pigs are particularly numerous in the northern tropics, here in Kakadu National Park. (KS/FLPA)

INTRODUCED MAMMALS

About 22 non-native mammal species have become established in the wild since being introduced by Europeans. A few, which are likely to be seen, are mentioned briefly here. Their effect on the environment is described earlier (see *Introduced bullies*, page 12).

The red fox (*Vulpes vulpes*) is found virtually everywhere except for the far north. Unfortunately, individuals have recently been reported on formerly fox-free Tasmania. It is slender and reddish brown, with pointed ears and a bushy tail. The European rabbit (*Oryctolagus cuniculus*), with its long ears and short white tail, is one of the most abundant and widespread mammals. The brown hare (*Lepus capensis*) is about twice its size, with longer ears, and is found mostly in the southeast and parts of Tasmania. The house mouse (*Mus musculus*) is found all over Australia, sometimes in plague proportions in grain-growing areas, and the black rat (*Rattus rattus*) in moister, coastal fringes, around human populations.

The goat (*Capra hircus*) has spread to every state, herds frequenting rocky or hilly, semi-arid areas. A brumby is a feral horse (*Equus caballus*). It is most common in the centre and north but herds roam sub-alpine pastures as well as semi-arid rangelands and the wetlands of Kakadu. The donkey (*E. asinus*) prefers tropical savanna and arid hill country; an estimated five million are wild. Australia is now the only place in the world where the one-humped camel (*Camelus dromedarius*) lives wild. It is descended from beasts of burden that were turned loose with the advent of rail and motor transport. Over a million camels roam arid areas, about half of them in Western Australia, and numbers are increasing rapidly, leading to controversial culls. The feral pig (*Sus scrofa*) is a large, stocky and potentially aggressive animal with a black or brown coat. Boars have long, curved tusks. It survives anywhere there is water and populations are particularly dense around wetlands. There are small populations of various deer species, particularly in the southeast. The fallow deer (*Dama dama*) is locally common in central Tasmania and the red deer (*Cervus elaphus*) – found in Victoria's Grampians and in southeast Queensland – appears on the latter state's crest.

Birds

Rainbow lorikeets are a common – and colourful – sight. (IM)

While Australia's mammals can be secretive, the birds are often visible, colourful, noisy and entertaining. Over 780 species have been recorded, close to half of them endemic or found only in Australia and New Guinea. Many are migratory, moving routinely within Australia, or overseas – to New Guinea, Asia and the northern hemisphere – according to season. However, about one-third are nomadic, moving opportunistically in response to Australia's unpredictable drought and flood conditions.

The following account describes most of the bird families found in Australia. It does not always follow a strict taxonomic order, with some birds grouped according to affinities of habitat and behaviour.

SEABIRDS

Seabirds are found in oceanic and coastal waters, although some gulls and terns also frequent inland water sources and may be seen far from the sea. The great ocean wanderers can travel vast distances, perhaps using the stars or the earth's magnetic field to navigate, and may only return to land to breed.

A short-tailed shearwater skims over the waves in search of food. (IM)

ALBATROSSES, SHEARWATERS, PETRELS AND PRIONS

Nine species of albatross (Diomedeidae) are recorded from Australian seas. These huge seabirds are seen most frequently along southern coasts in winter, riding the westerly winds on stiff, narrow wings, although anyone willing to brave the oceans on a pelagic bird-spotting trip is likely to see a variety at any time of year. The three smaller 'mollymawk' species are the most common, travelling as far north as the tropics; one of these, the shy albatross (*Diomedea cauta*), breeds around Tasmania between September and April.

Shearwaters, petrels and prions (Procellariidae), like albatrosses, have an excellent sense of smell and are able to detect food many kilometres away. They are mainly southern ocean birds and spend most of their lives at sea, flying close to the waves and diving and swimming underwater after prey. Most prions have fine bristle-like combs on their bills that enable them to sieve plankton from the ocean. The short-tailed shearwater (*Puffinus tenuirostris*) is one of the most numerous birds in the world. An estimated 23 million migrate from the northern hemisphere to breed in Australia (80% of them in Tasmania), making a round trip of 30,000km. The chicks of this species, also known as the muttonbird, are still legally harvested for food. Breeding colonies are a spectacle on summer evenings as circling parent birds return to their burrows at dusk. The wedge-tailed shearwater (*P. pacificus*) nests in colonies, mainly on tropical islands.

GANNETS, BOOBIES AND FRIGATEBIRDS

Gannets and boobies are similar-looking large seabirds that belong to the same family (Sulidae), the former living in southern, temperate oceans and the latter in the tropics. Most species are white with black wing markings, but some boobies are largely brown. Both plunge-dive spectacularly for food, air sacs under their skin cushioning the blow. Large numbers gather in noisy, smelly breeding colonies, where they incubate their eggs under their webbed feet.

The brown booby (*Sula leucogaster*) forages relatively close to shore. (IM)

Frigatebirds (*Fregata* spp) are tropical pirates. Superb aerialists, these large birds regularly hassle gulls, terns and boobies, forcing them to drop their food and catching it before it hits the water. Lacking waterproof feathers, they cannot dive for food, but can catch flying-fishes. Frigatebirds are mostly black, with long wings and long forked tails. Males have a scarlet throat pouch, which they inflate to impress females at breeding time.

The little penguin is an Australian resident. (EW/FLPA)

PENGUINS

The world's smallest penguin, the little penguin (*Eudyptula minor*), nests in short burrows or under dense vegetation around southern coastlines. Also known as the fairy penguin, it stands about 40cm high and has a dark back and white front, which makes it hard to see in the water, either from above or below. Colony numbers vary from a few pairs to over a thousand. The birds gather offshore at dusk, waddling ashore in groups under cover of darkness. Ten other penguin species visit, usually as vagrants.

GULLS AND TERNS

The silver gull (*Larus novaehollandiae*) is very common, especially around urban centres, where it scavenges food scraps. Its numbers have multiplied 1,000-fold in the last 50 years and, as a predator of eggs, it poses a serious threat to other species. This relatively small gull can turn up anywhere in Australia, ranging far inland if water is available. The much larger Pacific gull (*L. pacificus*), with a black back and a red spot on the end of its yellow bill, is common around the southern coasts. The similar kelp gull (*L. dominicanus*) has more white on the wing edge and a red spot just on the lower bill tip. It may have moved in from New Zealand and has a patchy, southerly distribution. Juveniles of both species are dark brown for the first couple of years. Terns, from the same family (Laridae), are slimmer birds with narrower wings and, generally, forked tails. Most are white with grey backs and, when breeding, black caps. They fly gracefully or hover, plunging dramatically into the water to seize prey. Noddies are blackish-brown tropical terns that pick up food from the water's surface.

Common noddies (*Anous stolidus*) breed in large colonies on islands and cays. (IM)

WATERBIRDS

A large and diverse group of birds is generally associated with water. Some are seen only in fresh water while others are equally at home in salt or fresh water – and in nearby grasslands. Some are resident but many are nomadic or migrate vast distances.

PELICAN, CORMORANTS AND DARTER

The Australian pelican (*Pelecanus conspicillatus*), an unmistakable, large, black and white bird with an enormous pink, pouched bill, is found in fresh and salt water throughout Australia, except for the most arid interior. You may see it circling high on thermals or cruising the shallows, alone or practising a little synchronised fishing with mates. Moving forward as a flotilla, the birds suddenly, in unison, plunge their enormous bills into the water, herding and trapping confused prey. When rare rains bring inland waterways to life, 40,000–60,000 pelicans can suddenly turn up, en masse, to breed. Their bills then turn a vivid orange-pink.

Five species of cormorant (Phalacrocoracidae) – medium to large black or black and white birds – occur in fresh or coastal waters. The plumage of these long-necked fishers is not waterproof, the saturated feathers reducing buoyancy, thus allowing them to swim

The pelican scoops up water and fish with its enormous bill pouch. (IM)

easily underwater in pursuit of fish. Trapping the victim in their long, hooked bill, they bring it to the surface, manipulate it deftly and swallow. These birds spend much of their time perched with wings open. While this allows the feathers to dry, it is also thought to aid digestion. Cormorants sometimes co-operate, occasionally with pelicans, to corral fish into shallows.

The darter (*Anhinga melanogaster*) resembles a cross between a cormorant and a heron. It pursues fish underwater then shoots out its kinked neck to spear the target with a long, thin beak. Like a cormorant it stands on a branch with wings spread, striking a familiar pose along many mainland waterways. The darter is also called 'snakebird' for its S-shaped neck, often the only thing showing above the surface when it swims.

HERONS, EGRETS, IBISES AND SPOONBILLS

Herons and egrets (Ardeidae) are common in wetlands. Long-legged stalkers, they patiently gaze into the water, specialised vertebrae allowing them to straighten their long, curved necks with lightning speed to spear aquatic prey. The white-faced heron (*Egretta novaehollandiae*) is particularly common. It has grey plumage – apart from its white face – and yellow legs. Egrets are mostly white, though the cattle egret (*Ardea ibis*), often seen in fields and feeding around livestock, develops orange-buff plumes around the head at breeding time. The eastern reef egret (*Egretta sacra*), common on most mainland coasts, comes in two forms – pure white or grey – sometimes from the same nest. The nankeen

Darters (left, IM) often perch with wings spread. White-faced herons (right, IM) are seen throughout Australia.

night heron (*Nycticorax caledonicus*) generally hunts at night and roosts in colonies by day. It has a shorter neck and legs than other herons. Five bittern species, from the same family, are shy, cryptically camouflaged and rarely seen.

Ibises (Threskiornithidae) can turn up quite suddenly in large numbers, appearing on the coast when the inland dries, or gathering in huge numbers to nest in response to inland flooding. Others are sedentary, even a nuisance in urban areas where they snatch food from outdoor tables. They forage on the edges of wetlands and in cultivated areas, snapping up aquatic prey and insects with long, curved beaks. Ibises fly in V-formations and gather in noisy treetop roosts. Of the three species, only the widespread straw-necked ibis (*Threskiornis spinicollis*) is endemic. The two species of spoonbill (*Platalea* spp) have white plumage, one with a yellow bill and legs and the other black. In waterways they often associate with ibises, scything their bills from side to side to trap prey in the spatulate tip.

A jabiru mingles with egrets, ibises and spoonbills. (IM)

STORK AND CRANES

The black-necked stork (*Ephippiorhynchus asiaticus*), Australia's only species, is often referred to as the jabiru, a Portuguese term for stork, though it is not the same as the South American species of the same name. This elegant bird is a distinctive feature of tropical wetlands where, usually alone, it probes the water with its massive bill. Standing well over a metre tall, it has a glossy green-black head and neck, black and white wings and long red legs. Pairs build huge, untidy nests of sticks.

The brolga has a dark dewlap under its chin. (TA/FLPA)

Two cranes (Gruidae) inhabit Australia. Both reach 1.4m in height and are light grey with bare red skin on the head. The brolga (*Grus rubicunda*) gathers in very large numbers across the north of the continent and, less commonly, in the east. Because the sarus crane (*G. antigone*) is so similar in appearance, there is confusion as to whether it arrived in the 1960s, when it was first recorded, or was simply previously overlooked. In the sarus, the red skin extends further down the neck and the legs are also red. It has a more restricted northerly distribution, where it often mixes with brolgas at roosts. These cranes are an impressive sight as they fly overhead honking, in V-formation, bounding as they land in massive, post-breeding congregations and sometimes lifting their wings and heads in exuberant dances.

WATERFOWL
Swan, ducks and geese

Europeans were highly sceptical when they heard of black swans (*Cygnus atratus*) in Australia. Certainly, to new arrivals, it must have been proof that they were in a topsy-turvy land. This lovely bird has white wing tips but these are generally hidden until it takes flight. It is found in salt and fresh water in most parts of Australia.

Also in the family Anatidae are about 20 native ducks and geese. The grey teal (*Anas gracilis*) is highly nomadic, following floods throughout the country. The Pacific black duck (*A. superciliosa*), a similar grey-brown bird but with bold black stripes on its head, is also

The black swan is the faunal emblem of Western Australia. (IM)

very widespread and often lives in public parks. It closely resembles the female of the introduced mallard (*A. platyrhynchos*) and the two have interbred to produce a hybrid. The Australian wood duck (*Chenonetta jubata*), a large grey duck with a brown head and speckled front, grazes like a goose, pairs usually sticking together. It nests in tree hollows, using claws on its feet for purchase. The ducklings jump to the ground not long after hatching. The plumed whistling-duck (*Dendrocygna eytoni*), named for the upswept plumes on its flanks and the sound of its shrill call is another grazer. Large numbers flock near water by day but at night fly off to feed in grasslands. The wandering whistling-duck (*D. arcuata*), by contrast, rarely leaves water, feeding in very large numbers in tropical wetlands. The Australian shelduck (*Tadorna tadornoides*) is an attractive black and chestnut bird of temperate wetlands that forms flocks of many hundreds outside the breeding season. The green pygmy-goose (*Nettapus pulchellus*) cruises among waterlilies in northern waterways. This small duck has a pretty green back and barred white-and-black front.

The magpie goose has a distinctive knob on its head. (IM)

The magpie goose (*Anseranas semipalmata*) is the only member of the Anseranatidae family; unlike other waterfowl its clawed feet are just partially webbed. With black and white plumage, red legs and beak, it is a distinctive bird of northern wetlands. Massive numbers congregate in swamps during the dry season, shuffling through the mud to find bulkuru tubers. During the breeding season (March to June) they switch to wild rice.

Grebes

Grebes, at first glance, look and behave like ducks. But they lack the flat bill, have lobed rather than webbed feet, and belong to a different and more ancient family (Podicipedidae). The Australasian grebe (*Tachybaptus novaehollandiae*), the smallest waterfowl, is common in fresh water. It dives deeply to chase fish and invertebrates, bobbing up like a cork only to disappear again. It flies poorly and rarely. The uncommon great-crested grebe (*Podiceps cristatus*) is much larger, with a characteristic neck-frill, crested head and elaborate courtship displays. Some grebes eat their own feathers and then feed them to their chicks, possibly to protect their stomachs from sharp fish bones.

The buff-banded rail is sometimes seen in the open. (IM)

COOTS, RAILS AND JACANAS

Birds in the Rallidae family tend to be plump in general appearance, with short upturned tails, which they flick repeatedly, and very large feet with long toes. Frequenting the swampy edges of waterways, most keep out of sight, but there are exceptions. The dusky moorhen (*Gallinula tenebrosa*) and the Eurasian coot (*Fulica atra*) are common in fresh water. Both are black, the moorhen with a red bill and shield (a fleshy patch on the forehead), the coot with white. The moorhen is a communal nester, males and females within a group practising free love and laying their eggs together in one nest. The colourful purple swamphen (*Porphyrio porphyrio*) prefers clambering to swimming and can be seen in waterside vegetation. The buff-banded rail (*Gallirallus philippensis*) is usually shy, but on some Queensland islands has become very numerous and extremely tame, stealing picnic lunches and bathing beside tourists. The Tasmanian native-hen (*Gallinula mortierii*) is a familiar sight throughout the island, with groups feeding in paddocks. It is able to run at 50km/h and has 14 different and eccentric calls, including a weird, cacophonous sawing sound produced by several birds.

Comb-crested jacana. (IM)

The comb-crested jacana (*Irediparra gallinacea*) belongs to a separate family, the Jacanidae. It is sometimes known as the lotusbird, lily-trotter or Jesus-bird because its enormously long-toed feet allow it to stroll across floating vegetation, apparently walking on water. It even nests on water. The larger female is boss, with up to five males in her territory dutifully caring for the eggs and chicks. Both sexes can change the colour of the fleshy comb on the front of their heads from red to yellow, according to mood.

WADERS (SHOREBIRDS)

Eighteen species of these birds reside in Australia, but at least 36 migratory species treat the place as a regular holiday destination and a further 21 vagrants turn up occasionally.

Sandpipers and allies

An estimated two million waders fly as much as 12,000km from breeding grounds in the Arctic each year to enjoy a life of perpetual summer. Most are members of the Scolopacidae family, including knots, godwits, curlews, sandpipers and stints. They start arriving in September and stay until about March, feeding together on mudflats and shorelines. Large numbers of arrivals and departures can be seen near Broome, the Gulf of Carpentaria and along the eastern Queensland coast. Some venture inland and a few non-breeders opt to sit out the southern winter. In their drab, non-breeding plumage, these largely brown and white birds are very difficult to tell apart, especially without a telescope, but bill shape can help. The eastern curlew (*Numenius madagascariensis*) is the largest, with a very long, curved bill. The whimbrel (*N. phaeopus*) is smaller, with a shorter, rather less curved, bill. The bar-tailed godwit (*Limosa lapponica*) has a long, slightly upturned bill, and often forms flocks of thousands that fly around in close formation. The red-necked stint (*Calidris ruficollis*) is one of the smallest and most numerous; close-knit flocks fly in unison and run around the shallows, jabbing the mud with their bills like sewing machine needles. The ruddy turnstone (*Arenaria interpres*) scampers along the shore turning over stones and pushing through seaweed in search of prey.

Plovers and allies

Plovers, dotterels and lapwings (Charadriidae) have much shorter bills than other waders and a few never wade. Some plovers are fairly large but the most familiar, like dotterels, are smallish, dumpy birds that run along shorelines, stopping suddenly to jab at prey. Most plovers migrate to the northern hemisphere to breed, but the double-banded plover (*Charadrius bicinctus*) goes to New Zealand instead, returning to Australia in winter. A few stay at home. The

A nesting red-capped plover feigns a broken wing to distract a predator. (IM)

widespread red-capped plover (*C. ruficapillus*) nests in a scrape in the sand or shingle; adults put on an impressive 'wounded bird' act if you go too close, which aims to lure potential predators away from the camouflaged eggs. The masked lapwing (*Vanellus miles*), with its upright stance, yellow facial wattles and harsh, staccato call, is a familiar resident of open areas. When nesting, it dive-bombs intruders and can defend itself with sharp, bony spurs sticking out from its shoulders; it is sometimes called the spur-winged plover.

Only when breeding do banded stilts sport a chestnut breastband. (IM)

Stilts, avocets and oystercatchers

Stilts are elegant, largely black and white birds, with exceptionally long, pink legs. The banded stilt (*Cladorhynchus leucocephalus*) is a resident species that moves and breeds opportunistically according to rainfall. Huge numbers may arrive at ephemeral saline lakes far inland to exploit the brine shrimp. How they know these lakes have filled, thousands of kilometres away, is a mystery. The red-necked avocet (*Recurvirostra novaehollandiae*) is similarly elegant, and has an upturned bill that it sweeps from side to side while wading. The pied oystercatcher (*Haematopus longirostris*), also black and white, has a long red bill for opening shellfish. It is common on beaches, particularly in the south, whereas the all black, and less common, sooty oystercatcher (*H. fuliginosus*) prefers rocky coasts.

The bush stone-curlew is commonly called the bush thick-knee. (IM)

Stone-curlews and pratincoles

The wailing call of the bush stone-curlew (*Burhinus grallarius*) is a familiar nocturnal sound in the north, where this bird is a common resident – though it is now rare in the southeast. Well camouflaged in brown, with long legs and large eyes, it lurks under cover by day – often in quite public places – and at night feeds in open areas. Although pratincoles (*Glareolidae*) run like waders, they fly gracefully like terns or swallows on narrow, pointed wings and catch insects on the wing. The Australian pratincole (*Stiltia isabella*) is fairly widespread and, of Australia's two species, the only one that breeds in the country.

GROUND BIRDS

This is a convenient category for some species that spend their lives on the ground but are not tied to water bodies. They have strong legs and usually run fast, being either unable – or reluctant – to fly.

EMU AND CASSOWARY

These two enormous, flightless birds can both stand almost 2m tall. Their double-shafted feathers lack the barbed filaments and stiffened structure found in those of flying birds, which gives cassowary plumage a hair-like appearance while the emu looks unkempt and shaggy. Males take full responsibility for the young. They brood the eggs constantly for seven or eight weeks, barely eating or drinking, and then look after the juveniles for up to 18 months (emu) or nine months (cassowary).

Emu

The emu (*Dromaius novaehollandiae*) is the slightly larger of the two. Common on arid plains and woodlands throughout the mainland, it has long, powerful legs and can sprint at 50km/h. Emus move nomadically, according to weather patterns. They cover large distances in their search for food, which consists of vegetation and invertebrates, but are sometimes blocked by artificial barriers causing thousands to perish. At breeding time the

Nomadic emus may travel great distances in search of food. (IM)

female dominates, inflating her throat pouch to make a booming sound that can be heard 2km away. She can lay up to 20 eggs but the male frequently chases her away after the seventh so she may mate with other males and lay in other nests. Relationships are complicated – tests have shown that as many as half the eggs in a clutch are not fathered by the brooding male. Emus like to bathe, even entering the sea to do so.

The southern cassowary. (IM)

Southern cassowary

The bizarre-looking southern cassowary (*Casuarius casuarius*) is confined to the tropical rainforests of north Queensland. It has black feathers and the bare skin of its head, neck and wattles is bright blue and red. The prominent casque on its crown is not horn or bone, as frequently stated, but formed from tough skin with a core of firm, cellular material. It may indicate age and status. Each dinosaur-like foot is furnished with a long, dagger-like middle toe, which it uses defensively, jumping up and kicking forward. Cassowaries are known as the

Despite its size and bright colours, a cassowary is hard to spot in the forest. (IM)

'gardeners of the forest' because they eat a variety of fruits and distribute the seeds, which are deposited in a pile of half-digested dung – a good sign of their presence. This shy bird is now endangered, due to habitat loss and other human pressures, but there are still places where you can see them reasonably easily, notably the Mission Beach area. Individuals used to being (illegally) fed can become demanding.

AUSTRALIAN BUSTARD

The Australian bustard (*Ardeotis australis*) – sometimes called the plains turkey – is one of the world's heaviest flying birds. The larger male can stand to 1.5m tall, with a wingspan of over 2m, and is an impressive sight as he strides deliberately through the grasslands. During courtship displays he puffs up his throat and fans out his neck and tail feathers. The dowdier female takes on all the child-raising duties. There are good numbers of bustards across the north, but in southern areas they have declined drastically since European settlement.

The male Australian bustard has a black breastband. (IM)

MOUND BUILDERS

Three species of chicken-like megapodes ('big foot') live in Australia, scratching through leaf-litter for food and building massive nesting mounds of vegetation and soil or sand. The decomposing vegetation generates heat, which incubates eggs laid in the mound. The adults (usually the male) regulate the temperature of the mound, keeping it at an optimum 33–34°C by adding or removing vegetation or digging ventilation holes as required. The big eggs contain large yolks and produce well-developed chicks that are completely independent when they emerge. All megapodes can fly, flapping heavily up on to tree branches to roost.

The Australian brush-turkey (*Alectura lathami*) is often encountered in east coast forests, where it visits picnic sites for handouts. Known affectionately as the 'bush chook' (chicken), it is black with a naked red head and yellow neck wattle that – in the male – dangles like a badly fried egg. The orange-footed scrubfowl (*Megapodius reinwardt*), from northern and eastern tropical coasts, is smaller but builds the biggest mound – up to 3m high. This odd-looking, dark-coloured bird has a triangular crest and outsized orange legs and feet. In the

A male Australian brush-turkey can retract its dangling wattle. (IM)

winter breeding season it calls loudly at night. The malleefowl (*Leipoa ocellata*), from dry, southern areas, is becoming scarce due to agricultural encroachment. Since egg-laying is affected by rainfall, numbers also suffer during droughts.

RAPTORS

Raptors are hunting birds that use talons to seize their prey and strong, hooked beaks to tear it apart. Apart from six falcon species (Falconidae), all Australian raptors belong to the Accipitridae family.

EAGLES

The massive wedge-tailed eagle (*Aquila audax*), with a wingspan of up to 2.5m, is Australia's largest bird of prey. Brown as a juvenile, it becomes darker with age. The 'wedgie' ranges across the whole country, feeding largely on carrion. This includes roadkill – although unfortunately, as it is slow to take off, the eagle itself sometimes becomes a casualty.

The wedge-tailed eagle is one of the world's largest raptors. (MW/FLPA)

The white-bellied sea-eagle (*Haliaeetus leucogaster*), with its grey back and white front, is easy to spot soaring or perching in coastal areas and inland waterways. It hunts fish, sea snakes, flying-foxes and waterfowl.

The black kite is commonly seen circling. (IM)

KITES

The black kite (*Milvus migrans*), distinguished by its forked tail, is also known as the fire hawk. Large numbers wheel around bushfires preying on escaping animals, and anecdotal evidence suggests they spread fires by picking up and dropping burning sticks. Whether this is deliberate or not is disputed, but these birds have certainly been observed luring fish to the water surface by dropping scraps of bread into a river. Large flocks also gather at locust swarms and rubbish tips. The common, but less gregarious, whistling kite (*Haliastur sphenurus*), has a lighter underwing pattern. The brahminy kite (*H. indus*) is a beautiful bird, with a chestnut-brown back and white head and front, that soars over tropical coastlines. The black-shouldered kite (*Elanus axillaris*) perches in the open and often hovers above prey.

HAWKS, HARRIERS AND OSPREY

The grey goshawk (*Accipiter novaehollandiae*) comes in two forms, one with a grey back and white front, the other pure white. It inhabits fairly dense forests and preys mainly on smaller birds, whose alarm calls are a good sign that one is about. The brown goshawk (*A. fasciatus*) lives in more open country but, being a stealth attacker of mammals and birds, likes some cover. Harriers drift across open vegetation on upswept wings, lowering their long legs to adjust direction or snatch startled prey. The spotted harrier (*Circus assimilis*) prefers more arid country of the mainland and the swamp harrier (*C. approximans*) the wetter areas, including Tasmania. The osprey (*Pandion haliaetus*) is one of the world's most widespread birds and is common around the coast. It targets fish, plunging into the water to snatch them from the surface. Pairs build massive stick nests.

The nankeen kestrel often perches in the open. (IM)

FALCONS

Falcons are small to medium-sized birds of prey, with a fast, agile flight on pointed wings. The peregrine falcon (*Falco peregrinus*) is the world's fastest animal, reaching speeds above 200km/h as it dives on other birds in mid-air. It is found virtually everywhere there are high cliffs and sometimes nests on tall buildings. The smaller Australian hobby (*F. longipennis*) perches in trees, watching for prey. It also feeds on birds, but at dusk may sally after bats and flying insects too. The nankeen kestrel (*F. cenchroides*), with rich brown back, hovers almost stationary before dropping on to prey on the ground.

PIGEONS AND DOVES

Australia's 22 native pigeons and doves (Columbidae) are diverse in appearance and behaviour. Ground-feeding seed-eaters tend to have fairly subdued plumage, some with an iridescent wing patch. The crested pigeon (*Ocyphaps lophotes*) has benefited from agricultural clearance, and is commonly seen running along the ground. The gentle 'doodle-do' call of the little peaceful dove (*Geopelia striata*) is a familiar sound in many mainland habitats except for the most arid.

The crested pigeon flies with a whistling wingbeat. (IM)

Fruit-eating species are generally more colourful and frequent the canopy. The pied imperial-pigeon (*Ducula bicolor*) is a large bird (up to 44cm) that migrates in great numbers to northern Australia in summer to breed. Mostly white, with black wing tips, it is conspicuous in flight, especially flocks commuting from nesting colonies. Three gorgeously plumaged fruit-doves can be surprisingly hard to spot in the trees. The rose-crowned fruit-dove (*Ptilinopus regina*), the most widespread, lives in forests and woodlands along much of the northern and eastern coasts while the aptly named superb fruit-dove (*P. superbus*) and the larger (up to 50cm) wompoo fruit-dove (*P. magnificus*) are found on the east coast. The latter is named for its call, which permeates its forest home.

PARROTS AND COCKATOOS

An impressive variety of parrots add colour, noise and character to the Australian landscape. With two toes pointing forward and two back, these birds can use their feet rather like hands to manipulate food, while their powerful hooked bill serves as an extra limb when clambering around trees. Some feed on nectar and pollen, others prefer fruit, and many raid the woody seed capsules of fire-prone plants. Most nest in tree hollows but two species use termite mounds. The majority of the 54 species are endemic.

Flocks of wild budgerigars call Australia home. (IM)

TRUE PARROTS

The family Psittacidae comprises the so-called 'true parrots' and includes such groups as the rosellas and lorikeets. One of the largest species is the Australian king-parrot (*Alisterus scapularis*), found in eastern forests, which has green wings and – in the male – a brilliant red body. The superficially similar red-winged parrot (*Aprosmictus erythropterus*) is more widespread throughout the north and east. Eastern and western ringnecks (*Barnardius* spp), the latter sometimes called Port Lincoln parrots or twenty-eights, are common in drier areas, particularly in Western Australia, where they frequently feed on the ground. The familiar budgerigar (*Melopsittacus undulatus*), which is green and yellow in its natural state, forms chattering, nomadic flocks. Careening swiftly and perching in trees, these appear almost anywhere in the interior after rain has produced flushes of seeding grasses.

Few birds are more colourful than the aptly named rainbow lorikeet (*Trichoglossus haematodus*), a common resident of eastern and southeastern coastal areas – with an orange-collared form found in the north. When quietly feeding in a tree this gaudy bird can prove surprisingly unobtrusive, but noisy flocks make themselves conspicuous, especially when gathering at evening roosts or feeding stations. The crimson rosella (*Platycercus elegans*) – one of several closely related blue-cheeked rosella species – is another bird that often approaches people for handouts. Adults are crimson and blue, while juveniles are largely green. Rosellas in another group have white or yellow cheeks.

Male Australian king-parrot. (IM)

Sulphur-crested cockatoo. (IM)

COCKATOOS AND GALAHS

Cockatoos, which belong to the family Cacatuidae, are generally loud, confident, gregarious birds with crests. The sulphur-crested cockatoo (*Cacatua galerita*) – the familiar white cage bird with the sassy, yellow headgear – is a home-grown Aussie hooligan. Big flocks feed on the ground or in trees, screeching raucously in flight and at roosts. When not feeding, these birds may idly prune branches and often peck destructively at human-built structures. The three species of corella (*Cacatua* spp) – smaller, predominately white cockatoos – are also highly gregarious.

Galahs are numerous in open country. (IM)

The galah (*C. roseicapilla*) has dark pink underparts, a lighter crest and grey back. Huge flocks, numbering up to a thousand, wheel noisily around their roost sites. This species is widespread throughout the drier country. Feeding on seed from the ground, like many cockatoos, it has benefited greatly from introduced grain crops. The red-tailed black-cockatoo (*Calyptorhynchus banksii*) is the most widespread of five similar species and particularly common across the northern savanna. All black-cockatoos are large (up to 65cm), the red, yellow or white in their tails contrasting with their black plumage. Usually in flocks, they fly with slow, lazy wingbeats, landing on branches that may sag under their weight. Food comprises mainly seeds in trees but also sometimes on the ground.

CUCKOOS AND COUCAL

Although two-thirds of the world's cuckoo species build their own nests, all Australian cuckoos (Cuculidae) are brood parasites, laying their eggs in the nests of over 100 different species and passing parental duties over to the duped, but dutiful, hosts. Many of the 13 Australian cuckoo species move south in spring to breed, heading back to northern Australia, and beyond, in winter. These inconspicuous birds are more often heard than seen, usually advertising their presence with loud, insistent calls.

Typical cuckoos are slim, medium-sized and greyish, but five smaller species of cuckoo, of which Horsfield's bronze-cuckoo (*Chrysococcyx basalis*) is the most widespread, have bronze-green backs and varying degrees of barring on their pale fronts and tails. Two large fruit-eating cuckoos migrate from Indonesia and New Guinea in spring, advertising their arrival with distinctive calls. The male common koel (*Eudynamys scolopacea*), named for its call, is black, but the female has a brown, white-spotted back and barred, buff underparts. The very large (66cm) channel-billed cuckoo (*Scythrops novaehollandiae*), with a massive 7cm-long bill, first appears in August. It has a crucifix silhouette in flight (the 'flying T-square') and calls raucously, often at night.

The pheasant coucal (*Centropus phasianinus*), once considered a cuckoo, has now been placed in the Centropodidae family. This large (70cm), chestnut-brown, pheasant-like bird, has a long tail and develops a black head and front when breeding. It skulks in low bushes, flies poorly and makes its own nest on the ground.

Horsfield's bronze-cuckoo forages for hairy caterpillars. (IM)

The barking owl also makes a human-like, wailing scream at mating time. (IM)

Tawny frogmouth. (IM)

BIRDS OF THE NIGHT

Although some diurnal birds are active also at night, especially when migrating, some birds specialise in nocturnal hunting. Excellent night-vision and other adaptations allow them to target prey that is hidden or inactive during the day.

OWLS

Owls are nocturnal raptors. Their soft plumage allows them to fly noiselessly and acute hearing enables them to home in on the faintest rustling of prey, which they catch in their powerful talons. Owls can be hard to find but some advertise their presence with their calls. The hawk-owl family (*Strigidae*) includes the southern boobook (*Ninox novaeseelandiae*), named for its often-repeated call (in New Zealand interpreted as 'morepork'), and the larger barking owl (*N. connivens*), which sounds just like a small dog. These two fairly common species are similar in appearance, with white-spotted wings and heavily streaked fronts. They roost in trees, where they may be mobbed by smaller birds, and sometimes hunt in daylight. Masked owls (Tytonidae) have large facial discs to concentrate the reception of sound. They tend to be more secretive. Sooty owls (*Tyto* spp) inhabit wet forests, picking off quite large possums and gliders. They produce a penetrating, descending 'falling-bomb' whistle.

FROGMOUTHS

Frogmouths (Podargidae) are nocturnal hunters. Although often confused with owls, they are more closely related to nightjars, and seize

The large-tailed nightjar (*Caprimulgus macrurus*) makes a call like wood-chopping. (IM)

their prey with broad, hooked bills, not with their feet. All three species share an ability to morph into dead branches: if disturbed when roosting, they close their eyes to a slit and lift their bills, their cryptic, streaked grey-brown plumage creating a perfect camouflage. Give every 'dead branch' a second glance! The tawny frogmouth (*Podargus strigoides*) is the most widespread.

NIGHTJARS

Nightjars (Caprimulgidae) are most often spotted flitting above the ground at dusk, as they hawk aerobatically for insects. The three species are hard to tell apart except by their often repetitive calls – or by location, the spotted nightjar (*Eurostopodus argus*) being more widespread in drier country. By day, nightjars roost on the ground, where their cryptic plumage provides perfect camouflage against the leaf-litter.

SWIFTS AND SWIFTLETS

These great aerialists (Apodidae) spend most of their lives flying. Despite their resemblance to swallows and martins, they are actually more closely related to nightjars and have a similarly wide gape for catching insects on the wing. The white-rumped swiftlet (*Collocalia spodiopygius*) of coastal Queensland nests and roosts in dense colonies in caves where, like insectivorous bats, it uses echolocation to navigate. The fork-tailed swift (*Apus pacificus*) forms large flocks that move across the country in summer. The white-throated needletail (*Hirundapus caudacutus*) is a large swift. One of the fastest in the world, reaching speeds of 130km/h, it sometimes passes with a startling whoosh and has been observed at heights of 2,000m. Although these swifts may sleep on the wing, circling high to do so, they also roost on trees and cliffs.

The fork-tailed swift breeds in the northern hemisphere. (IM)

Laughing kookaburras are always ready to share a joke.
(IM)

The azure kingfisher watches patiently for aquatic prey.
(IM)

KINGFISHERS

These attractive, generally colourful birds swoop on prey spotted from often quite exposed perches. Most nest in burrows or cavities.

KOOKABURRAS

Many people are surprised to learn that the laughing kookaburra (*Dacelo novaeguineae*) belongs to the kingfisher family (Halcyonidae). This large bird – it measures up to 47cm, including a robust 6cm bill – is predominately brown and white in colour. Common in the eastern mainland, and introduced to Western Australia and Tasmania, it is one of eight Australian kingfishers that feed away from water, swooping down from prominent vantage points on to insects, reptiles, small mammals and even other birds. Family groups start and end the day with a rollicking call as they proclaim their territory. The blue-winged kookaburra (*D. leachii*), which occupies northern and northeastern areas, is very similar but has more blue on wings and rump and produces a chorus of awful, maniacal screeching (it is also known as the howling jackass).

OTHER KINGFISHERS

The buff-breasted paradise-kingfisher (*Tanysiptera sylvia*) migrates in summer from New Guinea to breed on the Queensland coast; a medley of blue, white, orange and red, this birder's treat is encumbered with not only an unwieldy name but also a pair of 18cm-long white ribbons for a tail. Many kingfishers nest in arboreal termite mounds,

Rainbow bee-eaters are welcome summer visitors in the southern mainland. (IM)

opening up a hole with their powerful bills, but this species prefers rounded, free-standing mounds on the forest floor. The azure kingfisher (*Alcedo azurea*) is often glimpsed as a gorgeous flash of blue as it dashes along a stream. One of only two Australian river kingfishers (Alcedinidae), it nests in a burrow in the bank and dives for aquatic prey from an overhanging perch. The sacred kingfisher (*Todiramphus sanctus*), found in all but the most arid areas and Tasmania, is dark blue-green with pale underparts.

BEE-EATER AND DOLLARBIRD

The lovely rainbow bee-eater (*Merops ornatus*) is the only Australian member of its family (Meropidae). Blue and green, with long central tail shafts, it perches on telegraph wires and branches, and sallies after insects – bashing them loudly to remove their stings. Large, constantly chirruping flocks head south in spring and north in autumn, often travelling at night; in the north some are present all year. They nest communally in burrows that they excavate in sandy banks.

The dollarbird (*Eurystomus orientalis*), the sole representative of the roller family (Coraciidae) in Australia, migrates from New Guinea to northern and eastern Australia in summer. Mainly green and brown, it is most often seen as a dark, stocky silhouette high on a bare branch. When it swoops down to catch insects the pale 'silver dollar' spot on its wing is visible.

ALL IN THE FAMILY

Harsh conditions are thought to influence a common behaviour in Australian birds – co-operative breeding. From kookaburras and butcherbirds to honeyeaters, fairy-wrens and robins, more than 80 species breed in family groups, some unable to reproduce otherwise. Adolescent birds are not chased out of their parents' territory as they mature but spend years at home helping to incubate and feed the next generation. This reduces the strain on available resources in places where there is no seasonal spike in food availability, and also allows young birds time to hone foraging and parenting skills.

The rainbow pitta inhabits Top End and Kimberley forests. (IM)

SONGBIRDS

Almost half the bird species in Australia belong to the Passeriformes order, also known as 'songbirds' or 'perching birds'. This diverse group includes great songsters such as lyrebirds, whistlers, butcherbirds and magpies, as well as the vast honeyeater family and builders of bowers and exquisite nests.

PITTAS

Pittas (Pittidae) are dumpy ground-feeding birds whose elusive habits make them difficult to see, despite their brilliantly coloured plumage. The loud 'walk-to-work' call of the noisy pitta (*Pitta versicolor*) indicates its presence in summer in east coast rainforests, where it turns over leaf-litter while searching for snails and other invertebrates. It has electric-blue shoulder patches.

The male superb lyrebird is an outstanding show-off. (FL/FLPA)

LYREBIRDS

Lyrebirds (Menuridae) are restricted to Australia. With their ground-dwelling habits and impressive tails they recall a small pheasant. The males of both species are renowned for their extraordinary winter courtship displays. Strutting and prancing on their forest stages, they raise their trailing tail feathers over their backs and shake them, like shimmering fans, over their heads. This is accompanied by an outpouring of loud, liquid song, enriched by mimicry of other birds and sounds. The birds are named for the tail of the male superb lyrebird (*Menura novaehollandiae*), which resembles the musical instrument in shape. Females and juveniles have long, but less developed, trailing tails. During the summer, non-breeding, season the birds are much quieter, unobtrusively scratching for invertebrates on the forest floor.

MASTER MIMIC

A number of Australian birds are excellent mimics but the male lyrebird is the master. His song is considered the longest and most complex of all bird songs as he combines his own musical compositions with the perfectly mimicked songs of perhaps 20 other bird species. Mixed in are other sounds – barking dogs, car engines, camera shutters, burglar alarms, music and, sadly, chainsaws. The bird may

A superb lyrebird in full voice. (J&CS/FLPA)

perform for an hour at a time, for four hours a day. The female is also an excellent mimic; compared with European birds, a disproportionate number of Australian female birds sing, particularly in the tropics where they often duet with partners.

AUSTRALIAN TREECREEPERS

The seven members of the Climacteridae family (six in Australia and one in New Guinea) look and act rather like treecreepers (Certhiidae) elsewhere in the world. They are smallish, generally brown birds that work their way up the trunks of trees, probing the bark for insects (mainly ants) and then flying or gliding off to the base of another tree to start again. Unlike treecreepers elsewhere they shuffle, one foot at a time, instead of hopping, and do not support themselves with their tails. Unlike most birds they are able to climb along the lower sides of branches, although some species also forage extensively on the ground. Most nest co-operatively, the breeding pair assisted by one or two subordinate males, probably from a previous brood.

WRENS

Vigorous twittering in the undergrowth signals the presence of fairy-wrens (Maluridae). Most of these delightful little birds, with long, cheekily cocked tails, are grey-brown females, non-breeding males or juveniles – but males in full breeding plumage can be a stunning sight. The male splendid fairy-wren (*Malurus splendens*) more than earns his name; this little gem is a medley of luminous violet-, cobalt- and sky-blue with stripes of black. Most other males have some blue plumage, often combined with chestnut,

Splendid fairy-wren. (IM)

but others are red and black, black and white, or have a simple crown of purple. Fairy-wrens are co-operative breeders but genetic analysis has shown that free love is the rule; the female will mate with up to six different neighbouring males in addition to her partner, while the male is off (sometimes flower in beak) courting up to ten other females. Emu-wrens (*Stipiturus* spp), with very long but very thin tails (no bird has fewer tail feathers), are much more secretive birds of heathlands and spinifex. Grasswrens (*Amytornis* spp), well-camouflaged birds of spinifex and shrubby thickets, are similarly discreet.

The male spotted pardalote (*P. punctatus*) has a yellow throat. (IM)

PARDALOTES AND GERYGONES

Pardalotes (*Pardalotus* spp) are tiny warblers, brightly marked with spots and streaks. They have a stubby silhouette when moving through trees – often, for human observers, at neck-breaking height. Their short but broad bills are used to lever lerps and other insects from leaves.

Many of the other birds in this family (Pardalotidae) present a challenge to twitchers. Bristlebirds (*Dasyornis* spp) are rare, skulking, but relatively large heathland birds, with limited distributions.

Gerygones (*Gerygone* spp), pronounced 'jerriganee', were formerly known as fairy-warblers. The eight species are small, brown-grey birds, some with yellowish breasts, that flit around foliage, taking insects, and build globular or domed nests, some hanging above rivers and disguised as flood debris. Scrubwrens (*Sericornis* spp) are small brown birds, many with distinct eyebrows. They can be common in rainforest undergrowth and scrub. Thornbills (*Acanthiza* spp) are small, active, woodland birds, most of which have some streaking on the throat and breast.

HONEYEATERS AND CHATS

There are few places in Australia without at least some of the 72 honeyeater species (Meliphagidae). Using curved, pointed bills and partly tubular tongues with brush-like tips, these active birds feed predominantly on nectar and are important pollinators. Although they also eat insects and fruit, their reliance on nectar means that some species move nomadically with flowering and can be quite aggressive when competing for a resource. The majority of honeyeaters have brown, grey and/or yellow plumage but some are boldly patterned with black, white and red. Most are medium to small in size but tend to have loud calls; the machine-gun chatter of Lewin's honeyeater (*Meliphaga lewinii*) is a distinctive sound of east coast rainforests, while the brown honeyeater (*Lichmera indistincta*), a small, plain bird, produces a lovely, strong and varied song. The white-plumed honeyeater (*Lichenostomus penicillatus*) is one of the most widespread, small bands flitting through eucalypts to pick at the secretions of sap-sucking insects.

The tendency of many honeyeaters to live communally makes them conspicuous. The large, striking, blue-faced honeyeater (*Entomyzon cyanotis*), forms close-knit groups in forest

This yellow honeyeater (*Lichenostomus flavus*) is typical of its ubiquitous family. (IM)

fringes throughout the north and east. Miners take communal living to extremes. Hundreds of bell miners (*Manorina melanophrys*) take over tracts of forest, which ring with their chiming calls as if the forest were hung with bells – or supermarket checkout scanners. These birds feed on the sugary secretions of sap-sucking lerp insects but, since they do not harm the insects and aggressively chase away insectivorous birds, trees in the areas they occupy often suffer. The more widespread yellow-throated miner (*M. flavigula*), and the commonly encountered noisy miner (*M. melanocephala*) of the eastern mainland and Tasmania, also form complex social groups.

Wattlebirds and friarbirds are larger than the average honeyeater. The red wattlebird (*Anthochaera carunculata*), a common and conspicuous nomad in many habitats across southern and southeastern Australia, is named for the lobes of red skin on its cheeks. The noisy friarbird (*Philemon corniculatus*), known as the leatherhead for its dark, naked head, squabbles loudly over territory. Chats, also included in the honeyeater family, are mostly nomads of the arid zones, although the white-fronted chat (*Epthianura albifrons*) frequents open fields, heaths and coasts of the southern mainland and Tasmania.

THE BIRDS, NOT THE BEES

Australian birds play an important role as plant pollinators. Over 70 honeyeater and lorikeet species feed largely on nectar, and more than 1,000 plant species – including eucalypts, melaleucas, grevilleas and banksias – attract them with colourful flowers, copious nectar and sturdy branches to support their weight.

A male red-capped robin. (IM)

AUSTRALIAN 'ROBINS'

Although the 20 species of Australian robin (Petroicidae) are not related to the European 'red-breast', they are similarly plump-looking, perching birds. The males of some species have striking red or pink breasts with black, or black and white, heads and backs. Most are forest and woodland birds of the southeastern mainland and Tasmania, but the red-capped robin (*Petroica goodenovii*) prefers more arid habitats across the southern mainland. Other robins have yellow breasts. The eastern yellow robin (*Eopsaltria australis*), with its grey head and back, is very common in forests of the eastern mainland and, like many Australian robins, often perches sideways on tree trunks. Other robins are more subtly coloured in grey, brown, black and white. The jacky winter (*Microeca fascinans*) is a lively bird with fairly dull plumage and a habit of perching on fences in open areas.

LOGRUNNERS

There are just two Australian species in the Orthonychidae family. These energetic leaf-litter turners have a peculiar habit of leaning back on their tails and clearing debris with a sideways kick instead of one to the rear. Their strong tail feathers (12 instead of the usual ten) terminate in long spines. Fossil records show that these birds were once much more widespread, but the chowchilla (*Orthonyx spaldingii*) is now restricted to upland rainforests of north Queensland and the logrunner (*O. temminckii*) to southeastern forests. Both species are well camouflaged and rarely fly. Their very loud calls resound at dawn and dusk.

AUSTRALIAN BABBLERS

Gregarious, noisy birds of the Pomatostomidae family breed co-operatively, building large, untidy nests with side entrances. They forage together in dry woodlands and scrub, bounding along the ground, flying in short bursts and using their long, curved bills to probe crevices. The grey-crowned babbler (*Pomatostomus temporalis*) is the largest and most conspicuous of Australia's four species, but numbers are declining due to habitat destruction.

The white-browed babbler (*P. superciliosus*) inhabits the drier southern mainland. (IM)

WHIPBIRDS AND WEDGEBILLS

The call of the eastern whipbird (*Psophodes olivaceus*) is frequently heard in east coast forests. A thin note is followed by a loud 'whip crack', which the second bird of the pair concludes with a couple of chirrups. Olive brown, with a white throat and crest, this species forages on the forest floor, usually with a mate and, though loud, is often hard to see.

Belonging to the same family (Cinclosomatidae), the chiming wedgebill (*P. occidentalis*) is grey-brown with a distinct crest. It perches at the top of a shrub, in central and western arid areas, repeating its metallic, descending call. The chirruping wedgebill (*P. cristatus*) from eastern central districts is identical in appearance but has a different call.

WHISTLERS AND SHRIKE-THRUSHES

This is a family (Pachycephalidae) of fairly stout insectivores, with loud, often tuneful calls. The crested bellbird (*Oreoica gutturalis*) lives in lightly wooded areas of the arid zone, where it sings from treetops, broadcasting its liquid, ventriloquial song in all directions. The related whistlers (eight species) are renowned for their resonant, sometimes explosive songs. The rufous whistler (*Pachycephala rufiventris*), a widespread woodland species, works its way through foliage, feeding on insects. The male has a white throat encircled with black, a black head and a rufous breast. The male golden whistler (*P. pectoralis*) has a similar head pattern but with a brilliant yellow front and collar; the female is mainly dull grey-brown.

The male golden whistler, a bright spot in dense foliage. (IM)

Shrike-thrushes are medium-sized with mostly subdued, brownish plumage and loud calls. They are not related to thrushes or shrikes. The most widespread, the grey shrike-thrush (*Colluricincla harmonica*), hops through branches taking large insects and even nestlings and small mammals. The little shrike-thrush (*C. megarhyncha*) is found in northern and eastern Australia and New Guinea where, curiously, some have been found to contain toxins (batrachotoxins) similar to those in the secretions of poison dart frogs of Central and South America and possibly derived from eating particular beetles. It is unclear if Australian individuals are also poisonous.

MASTER BUILDERS

Songbirds are master nest builders. Many nests are tightly or smoothly bound – even felted – with cobwebs, and camouflaged with decorations such as lichens, moss, bark, flowers, caterpillar droppings, spiders' egg sacs and even living leaves stitched on with cobwebs. Cup or purse-shaped nests of many species, notably honeyeaters, are suspended by the rim from forked branches or from leafy branchlets too delicate to bear the weight of a predator. Others, such as gerygones and sunbirds, build dangling domes with side entrances.

The spectacled monarch weaves its nest around an upright fork. (IM)

The willie wagtail is constantly on the move, flushing insects. (IM)

FLYCATCHERS AND RELATIVES

This is a family (Dicruridae) of insectivorous birds, most with stout bills surrounded by bristles that help them catch prey. The leaden flycatcher (*Myiagra rubecula*) belongs to a group of slim, active birds with constantly quivering tails. The female, with a rufous throat, is brighter than the dark grey and white male. The harsh, rasping call of the spectacled monarch (*Monarcha trivirgatus*) draws attention to this lovely bird, with its rich rufous breast, grey back and black face. Like the similar black-faced monarch (*M. melanopsis*), it is a flycatcher of eastern forests.

The grey fantail (*Rhipidura fuliginosa*), one of the most common and widespread of five fantail species, is constantly on the move, fluttering and fanning its tail as it chases insects through the foliage. Another fantail, the black and white willie wagtail (*R. leucophrys*), is found almost everywhere and is one of Australia's most familiar birds. It hunts mainly on the ground, constantly fanning and waggling its tail. Tame, but feisty, it often harasses much larger birds. Rivals, flaring out their white eyebrows, dive at each other with loud, scolding chatters and on still summer nights their sweet songs can be heard competing from neighbouring territories.

The magpie-lark (*Grallina cyanoleuca*), also known as the peewee, is another very familiar and widespread bird. Boldly patterned in black and white, this very large flycatcher struts around on the ground feeding or collecting mud to build its nest. Pairs fly on to perches where, with open wings, they duet stridently. Magpie-larks and willie wagtails often nest close together, these two belligerent flycatchers joining forces to mob potential predators and sometimes even swooping on people.

The spangled drongo (*Dicrurus bracteatus*) is a glossy black bird with a long, forked tail and a discordant, twanging call – like a demented robot. It sallies aerobatically for insects from exposed perches, but sometimes also attacks small birds.

The spangled drongo is an assertive predator. (IM)

CUCKOO-SHRIKES AND TRILLERS

Birds in this family (Campephagidae) are more closely related to orioles than to cuckoos or shrikes, but have a cuckoo-like form and flight, and shrike-like bills. They are mostly grey and white with some barring, although some trillers are brown. Cuckoo-shrikes move from tree to tree, pouncing on insect prey and folding and refolding their wings on landing; the widespread black-faced cuckoo-shrike (*Coracina novaehollandiae*) is also called 'shufflewing'. The male white-winged triller (*Lalage suewii*) moults into black and white plumage about August when it moves south to breed. Back in the north for winter it becomes brown again, resembling the female.

ORIOLES AND FIGBIRD

Interbreeding creates figbirds with yellow and grey fronts. (IM)

Orioles are medium-sized, mainly fruit-eating birds, with yellow and green plumage and – especially in females and immatures – heavily streaked breasts. They have melodic, bubbling calls. The figbird (*Sphecotheres viridis*), also a member of the Oriolidae family, forms flocks along the eastern mainland coast and across the north. The male has a patch of red skin around his eyes that intensifies with excitement. Males in the north have yellow breasts and those in the south grey-green.

The pied butcherbird (*C. nigrogularis*) is a melodic predator. (IM)

WOODSWALLOWS, BUTCHERBIRDS AND ALLIES

The Artamidae family contains some unlikely siblings. Woodswallows have soft grey, brown and white plumage. They are unrelated to swallows but appear superficially similar as they soar into the air from vantage perches to snatch insects. They also use their brush-like tongues to collect nectar. Social birds, woodswallows gather in chirruping flocks and have an endearing habit of snuggling together, side-by-side. Five of the six Australian species are highly mobile, with a tendency to move south to breed in summer.

Butcherbirds (*Cracticus* spp) are black or pied birds, although juveniles are often brown or rufous. These stealthy hunters pounce on insects, reptiles, frogs, small birds and eggs, provoking outbursts of alarm calls from other birds when spotted. Wedging prey in a tree fork, they tear it apart with strong, hooked bills. Their pure, fluting songs are among the most atmospheric sounds of the Australian bush.

The amount of white on an Australian magpie's back varies with race. (IM)

An equally evocative sound is the carolling of the Australian magpie (*Gymnorhina tibicen*). This large, black and white bird is unrelated to the European magpie and spends much of its time strutting and probing the ground, often in company. It is very territorial and, when nesting, notorious for swooping at anyone who comes too close. Currawongs are large grey, black or pied birds with robust beaks and yellow eyes. The loud call of the pied currawong (*Strepera graculina*) is a characteristic sound of eastern forests. Large flocks wander nomadically, generally spending summers at higher altitudes and moving to the lowlands in winter.

Victoria's riflebird (*Ptiloris victoriae*), a treat for birders in Queensland's wet tropics. (IM)

BIRDS OF PARADISE

Four birds of paradise (Paradisaeidae) live in Australia. Three species of riflebird have fragmented distributions in the wet forests of coastal Queensland and New South Wales. The males are velvety black with metallic blue-green heads and throat shields, their plumage making a loud, rustling noise in flight. During the mating season a suitor displays on a high, exposed stump or branch. Opening his beak to show off his bright yellow mouth, he throws back his head, fans his wings in a circle over his body and thrusts out his breast feathers and iridescent throat shield. Swaying and shuddering, he rhythmically dips alternate wings as he encircles his mesmerised mate, who may join in the dance. She then goes off to nest alone while her suitor continues to advertise for more partners. Females have subdued brown and cream plumage and very long curved bills. The trumpet manucode (*Manucodia keraudrenii*) is a glossy, red-eyed, black bird of paradise found at the very top of Cape York Peninsula.

RAVENS, CROWS AND MUD-NEST BUILDERS

All five native crows and ravens (Corvidae) are black, with a large bill and pale eyes. Similar in size, they are hard to distinguish other than by distribution and calls. The white-winged chough (*Corcorax melanorhamphos*) looks superficially like a crow but has a large, white wing patch, visible in flight and, together with the apostlebird (*Struthidea cinerea*), belongs to the Corcoracidae family. Both species form tight-knit clans that forage on the ground in dry eastern woodlands and use mud to build large, durable, bowl-shaped nests plastered on to tree branches. Families co-operate to incubate and rear the young. Pairs of white-winged choughs are unable to reproduce successfully alone, needing up to ten in a group to raise all four chicks. This entails feeding youngsters for up to eight months after they have left the nest while they gradually hone their foraging skills. Groups will even kidnap young birds from other families to boost their future breeding chances. Early settlers thought apostlebirds always came by the dozen – hence the name – though numbers actually vary from six to 20. This medium-sized grey and brown bird has earned the nickname 'lousy Jack' among some Aboriginal people as its alarm calls often spoil the hunt.

Apostlebirds like company. (IM)

A hopeful male satin bowerbird peers out of his bower. (CR/FLPA)

BOWERBIRDS

Male bowerbirds (Ptilonorhynchidae) devote much of their energy to the art of seduction, building elaborate structures for the sole purpose of seducing females – which then build nests and rear the young alone. Most species make 'avenue bowers', which comprise two parallel walls of thin, upright twigs stuck in a foundation mat to form a curved U-shaped corridor, and are decorated with hundreds – even thousands – of objects, such as berries, shells, stones, glass, plastic and other human-made items. Competition is fierce between rival male bowerbirds, which sometimes destroy each other's bowers and steal ornaments. When a female approaches, the male dances, flutters and shows off his handiwork. If she is suitably impressed she will reward him, in the bower, with her favours.

The male satin bowerbird (*Ptilonorhynchus violaceus*), of wet, eastern districts, has glossy blue-black plumage. The duller female is olive-brown with scalloped underparts, but both sexes have brilliant blue eyes – the same hue as the decorations the male collects for his bower. This species can be very common in places (thanks perhaps to the abundance of blue, plastic, romance enhancers), female and immature birds forming large, winter flocks. The great bowerbird (*Chlamydera nuchalis*), very common across the north, builds substantial avenue bowers, usually under protective vegetation. The golden bowerbird (*Prionodura newtoniana*) from north Queensland upland rainforests, like its relatives in New Guinea, builds a maypole bower – twin or single towers of sticks, sometimes over 2m tall, constructed around and between adjacent saplings. A connecting or protruding display perch is decorated with lichens, fruits and flowers. The tooth-billed bowerbird (*Scenopoeetes dentirostris*) simply clears a courtship stage and decorates it daily with fresh leaves, but makes up for his lack of construction skills with a masterful mimicry of other birds' songs. Spotted and green catbirds (*Ailuroedus* spp) belong to the same family but do not build bowers. Their loud, harsh, drawn-out calls are a conspicuous feature of eastern rainforests.

GRASSFINCHES AND MANNIKINS

Members of the Passeridae family are busy, generally sociable birds. Most species are beautifully patterned in brown, black and white, and some with various amounts of bright red. They often move in twittering flocks, sometimes of mixed species, feeding mainly on seeds and insects and flying regularly to water. The zebra finch (*Taeniopygia guttata*) is the most familiar of several Australian species kept in cages all over the world. On its home turf it is widespread throughout the arid and semi-arid mainland. The male crimson finch (*Neochmia phaeton*), from northern districts, is almost entirely blood red, while firetail finches (*Stagonopleura* spp) are named for their flashy, scarlet rumps. The multi-coloured Gouldian finch (*Erythrura gouldiae*) is simply gorgeous, though sadly now rare due to habitat changes and disease. Immatures are much duller than adults and can be confusing.

Crimson finches forage nimbly on grass stems. (IM)

SUNBIRDS AND FLOWERPECKERS

Australia has one species each of these two largely tropical families. The yellow-bellied sunbird (*Nectarinia jugularis*) is a common garden bird of coastal northern Queensland, often building its pendulous nest near houses and in public places. Both sexes have olive-brown backs and yellow fronts but the male also has an iridescent black bib. These assertive little birds sometimes flit about in argumentative, twittering groups but may suddenly stop still, pointing beaks to the sky. They probe flowers for nectar with their long, curved bills and also pick up insects.

The mistletoebird (*Dicaeum hirundinaceum*), Australia's only flowerpecker, is common throughout the mainland anywhere there are mistletoes, its main food. The fruits pass quickly through its gut and are very sticky when excreted so the bird has a habit of wiping them off on tree branches where they later germinate; plants and birds thus share a mutual dependence. A sharp 'tzee' is usually the best indication of the bird's presence. The beautiful little male, with black back and scarlet throat and upper breast, is worth searching for. The more subdued female, like the male, has a red undertail.

Yellow-bellied sunbirds sip nectar and hover to pick spiders from webs. (IM)

SWALLOWS AND MARTINS

Swallows and martins (Hirundinidae) are a familiar sight as they swoop gracefully after insects. Unlike swifts, to which they are not related, these birds can perch, landing on wires and other supports where they can be observed more easily. They also tend to fly closer to the ground. Swallows have longer and more deeply forked tails than martins. Most species are partially migratory, or nomadic, tending to move north after breeding. The most familiar species, the welcome swallow (*Hirundo neoxena*), commonly nests under eaves and other human-made structures. It is very similar in appearance and habits to the barn swallow (*H. rustica*), which sometimes visits northern Australia from Asia. The fairy martin (*H. ariel*) builds a bottle-shaped mud nest, often in colonies under masonry structures.

Large flocks of silvereyes move from south to north in late summer. (IM)

WARBLERS AND WHITE-EYES

Many of the ten species of warbler (Sylviidae) are brownish and rather dull in appearance, so it is nice that one, the zitting cisticola (*Cisticola juncidis*), is in contention for most eccentric name. Most species are best identified by voice, and the clamorous reed-warbler (*Acrocephalus stentoreus*) is also very aptly named; with its rich, loud, liquid song, it is more often heard than seen. The two songlarks (*Cincloramphus* spp) in this group are not larks at all.

White-eyes are superficially similar to warblers, but all members of this unrelated family (Zosteropidae) are immediately distinguished by the conspicuous white circles around their eyes. There are three species in Australia, of which by far the most common is the silvereye (*Zosterops lateralis*). Flocks move rapidly through shrubs and trees, calling constantly – and distracting birdwatchers – as they seek insects, fruit and nectar. Plumage varies according to race in different parts of the country.

Metallic starlings are exceptionally social. (IM)

THRUSHES, STARLINGS AND MYNAS

Two introduced members of the Muscicapidae family have become established in Australia: the European blackbird (*Turdus merula*) throughout the southeast and Tasmania, and the song thrush (*T. philomelos*) in southern Victoria. Two near-identical native species, the russet-tailed thrush (*Zoothera heinei*) and Bassian thrush (*Z. lunulata*), are inconspicuous skulkers of the forest floor. Both have brown backs and whitish fronts beautifully scalloped with brown.

There is only one native member of the starling family (Sturnidae). The metallic starling (*Aplonis metallica*) of north Queensland breeds in noisy colonies, with dozens, sometimes hundreds, of bulky, fibrous nests suspended from the branches of the chosen tree – occasionally weighing it down to breaking point. Swift, twittering flocks hurtle between fruiting trees, miraculously avoiding cars and cyclists. Adults are glossy black, with purple and green iridescence, and have bulging red eyes. The duller adolescents have streaked white breasts. Most migrate to New Guinea in winter, but some stay all year. The introduced common starling (*Sturnus vulgaris*) is a pest of the southeast, including Tasmania. The common myna (*Acridotheres tristis*) from Asia is also a problem bird, occurring in patches along the east and southeastern mainland coast where it competes aggressively with native species for nesting hollows.

REPTILES

The amethystine python is
Australia's largest snake. (GW)

More than 860 reptile species have been described in Australia and many more are unnamed. Although most belong to families also found elsewhere in the world, isolation has produced many endemic species. The varied and generally warm habitats, particularly the hot, dry conditions of the arid zone, favour reptiles. Indeed, the Simpson Desert, which can support as many as 40 lizard species in just one square kilometre of spinifex, has perhaps the highest reptile diversity on earth.

Reptiles are energy-efficient creatures that use solar power to generate body heat and therefore need only about 10% as much food as mammals. If conditions are too cold or too hot, they can shut down and become inactive (aestivate). They are also very water-efficient, thanks to their waterproof skins – even the eyes of some lizards and snakes are capped with transparent, waterproof scales – and their ability to excrete urine as crystals rather than as a liquid. Male lizards and snakes have two penises, used alternately and kept within the body when not in use.

CROCODILES

Two crocodile species inhabit northern Australia. They are more often seen in winter when they spend periods of time basking in the sun to increase their body temperatures; slide marks on riverbanks are a sure sign of their presence.

ESTUARINE CROCODILE

The estuarine crocodile (*Crocodylus porosus*) is the largest reptile in the world, with the biggest males growing to over 6m long (though averaging closer to 4m) and unconfirmed reports of even larger. Its massive jaws close in a characteristic uneven line, leaving teeth visible even when shut. This species is found in southeast Asia and the tropical coastal

A large estuarine crocodile can weigh well over one tonne. (IM)

regions of northern Australia. Its alternative name of saltwater croc – or 'saltie' – is misleading, as many live in billabongs, swamps, lakes, rivers and other freshwater environments. Thanks to salt-excreting glands at the back of the tongue, however, it may also inhabit estuaries and offshore islands, and sometimes travels in the open sea.

STAY OFF THE MENU

The number of deaths from crocodile attack are minimal compared with road accidents, but they do occasionally happen. In the north assume that all natural waterways contain crocodiles. Do not swim or stand in water. Keep several metres away from the water's edge (including when fishing) and do not sit on overhanging branches or dangle legs or arms over the edge of boats. Never leave fish or food scraps near the water or at waterside campsites. Camp at least 50m from the water's edge and well above high tide level. Crocs are particularly active and mobile in the breeding season, between September and April, and often travel along coastlines. They also move with floodwaters during the wet season.

Young estuarine crocs eat invertebrates and crustaceans, moving on to fish, birds and small mammals as they grow. Large crocs can kill cattle, buffaloes, pigs, humans and anything else within reach. These huge reptiles conserve their energy by moving slowly. They can remain fully submerged for lengthy periods due to extremely efficient heart–lung–blood functions, but often float with just nose tip and eyes above the surface. This is a useful ambush strategy, allowing

Crocs cool down by opening their jaws to lose heat through the thin skin of the mouth and tongue. (MP/FLPA)

a croc to use its keen senses of smell, sight and hearing while most of its body lies hidden. When prey comes within reach, the croc bursts out of the water into the air or up the bank to grab it – closing its jaws with an immense crushing pressure that has been compared to the brakes on a jumbo jet. Twisting in a characteristic 'death roll', it drags its victim under water where it quickly drowns. Contrary to popular belief, crocodiles do not stash corpses underwater but prefer fresh food.

Female crocodiles lay their eggs in mounds of vegetation. Ideal incubation temperatures of around 32°C produce males. Higher and lower temperatures produce

Freshwater crocodiles are distinguished by their narrow, even jawlines. (IM)

more females. The mother defends her nest and, when the hatchlings begin to emerge, she gently helps open the eggs, carries the young to water in her mouth and protects them for several weeks. Nonetheless, fewer than 1% are likely to survive predation.

Researchers in Queensland have been astonished at the homing abilities of estuarine crocodiles. A number were captured, fitted with satellite transmitters, translocated and their movements tracked; all found their way home. The researchers then put one to the ultimate test. They flew it, by helicopter, from the west side of Cape York Peninsula to the east. Twenty days later it was home, having swum right around Australia's northern tip, a journey of more than 400km.

FRESHWATER CROCODILE

The freshwater crocodile (*Crocodylus johnstoni*) is found only in Australia and only in fresh water. It usually avoids competition from its larger cousin by staying upstream or in separate waterways. Rarely reaching 3m in length, 'freshies' are slimmer than salties, with narrower snouts and a more even jawline. This snout is well suited to catching fish, their main prey, along with frogs and other aquatic animals. Females nest in riverbanks during the dry season, returning to help the young when they hatch. Freshies do not eat people but have been known to bite, probably in self-defence or by mistake.

TURTLES

Turtles belong to an ancient order, Chelonia, which has changed little over the past 200 million years. All have shield-like shells, the carapace on top and the plastron below. Australia is home to marine and freshwater turtles but no land tortoises. See page 156 for more about marine species.

FRESHWATER TURTLES

There are about 25 described species of freshwater turtle in Australia, where they are often referred to, erroneously, as tortoises. With one exception, all belong to the Chelidae

Cann's long-necked turtle (*Chelodina canni*) releases a foul-smelling fluid when under stress. (IM)

family. Known as side-necked turtles, they withdraw their heads by folding their necks sideways under their carapaces and have webbed, clawed feet instead of flippers. Turtles can be common in fresh water, often basking on overhanging branches and sometimes paddling over to visitors anticipating a feed – although this is not good for their health. Some ('bum-breathers') are able to spend hours, even days, underwater by using the lining of the cloaca to extract oxygen.

Long-necked turtles have snake-like necks, sometimes longer than the carapace. The northern long-necked turtle (*Chelodina rugosa*) is common in the north, from Cape York Peninsula to the Kimberley, with adults growing to about 36cm in carapace length. At the beginning of the dry season it buries into the still-damp soil, which eventually bakes hard around it. The turtle remains in a state of torpor (aestivation) until rain softens the mud. Aboriginal people look out for telltale breathing holes and prod the mud; if the probe hits a turtle it is

The saw-shelled turtle is a common sight in Queensland waterways. (GW)

unearthed and cooked. Inundation commonly destroys reptile eggs but, uniquely, these turtles lay their eggs underwater. They do not begin to develop until the water level drops during the dry season, and hatch when the wet season brings more rain.

A number of species with necks of a more conventional length are found across the north and along the east coast. The saw-shelled turtle (*Wollumbinia latisternum*), of Queensland waterways, has a carapace of up to 28cm, with a serrated rear edge. The serrations are less obvious in older adults.

The centralian blue-tongued skink (*T. multifasciata*) is widely distributed in the arid zone. (GW)

LIZARDS

Lizards are an Australian speciality and, after birds, the most commonly seen vertebrates. Most have four well-developed limbs, although in some species these are not visible, sometimes leading to confusion with snakes. Unlike snakes, all lizards have external ear openings.

SKINKS

There are more than 370 species of skink (Scincidae) in Australia, making them the country's most diverse and numerous vertebrates. The majority are small (5–10cm), smooth and fast-moving. Most are diurnal and live on the ground, feeding mainly on invertebrates. They are generally fond of sunbathing but are quick to scuttle away when disturbed, although they often stop again and can be approached, cautiously, quite closely. Some can even see with their eyes shut, thanks to a transparent window in the lower eyelid. While most lizards lay eggs some skinks, particularly those in cooler climates, give birth to live young.

Rainbow skinks (*Carlia* spp) are particularly common in tropical Australia. Some have an iridescent sheen and the males may develop bright breeding colours, such as red flanks. These skinks often wave their tails sinuously, possibly as a form of communication. Over 95 species of striped skink (*Ctenotus* spp) are found throughout the mainland and are particularly diverse in spinifex deserts. They are boldly striped, often with spots. Most skinks of the *Egernia* genus are large and stout. The dark, glossy land mullet (*E. major*), which inhabits wet forests of the mid-east coast, grows to lengths of 58cm.

Blue-tongued skinks, if threatened, open their pink mouths and stick out their large, contrasting, blue tongues while hissing and inflating their bodies. Often found in parks and gardens, they usually move slowly – though they can sprint – and, like many of the larger skinks, eat vegetable matter and slow-moving invertebrates. A very distinctive blue-tongue, the shingleback (*Tiliqua rugosa*), is also known as the bobtail, stumpy tail, pinecone or sleepy lizard. It weighs up to 1kg and measures up to 30cm in body length, with a short, blunt tail and very large, thick scales. This species is widespread in southern Australia, west of the Great Dividing Range, in open habitats. Individuals may live for 20 years or more and pairs mate for life, meeting up each spring to breed. The common blue-tongue (*T. scincoides*), with a total length of 60cm, is one of the world's largest skinks.

GECKOS

There are over 110 gecko (Gekkonidae) species in Australia. Most are small, soft-skinned, nocturnal lizards with large eyes, which generally hide away under tree bark or similar crevices by day. They use the warmth of these retreats, or warmed surfaces, to raise their body temperatures. Some are pale at night and darker during

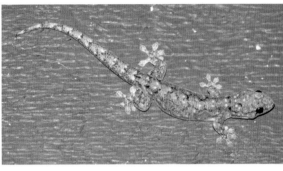

Native dtella geckos (*Gehyra* sp.) are common residents of houses. (IM)

the day. Unlike most lizards, geckos are able to vocalise. They also lick their eyes with their tongues. A few species exist only as females, producing female clones without mating. When threatened, like some skinks, geckos readily drop their tails, which continue to wriggle, distracting predators while the owner escapes. The tails grow back, with cartilage replacing the lost vertebrae.

Most tropical dwellings have a resident population of geckos stationed around lights at night, advancing to pounce on confused moths and other invertebrates. The Asian house gecko (*Hemidactylus frenatus*), a common, introduced species that probably hitched a ride on cargo boats, has a distinctive, loud, scolding call. Australia's most widespread native species, Bynoe's gecko (*Heteronotia binoei*), lives in dry, open areas. It is about 10cm long, with irregular bands and spots of brown, black and white. Females, some of which reproduce without males, often lay in communal nests containing up to 150 eggs.

A number of knob-tailed geckos (*Nephrurus* spp), with strangely shrunken tails ending in a round ball, are found throughout the mainland. The heaviest, the centralian knob-tailed gecko (*N. amyae*), is found only in rocky areas around Alice Springs, where it is quite common along road verges on summer nights. Leaf-tailed geckos (*Saltuarius* and *Phyllurus* spp) have flat bodies with laterally expanded tails. Their lichen-like colours and patterns, and flat, shadow-free profiles camouflage them magnificently on trees and rocks. They are

Leaf-tailed geckos are relatively large, but very difficult to spot. (GW)

restricted to the rainforests of Queensland and New South Wales. Many species in the *Diplodactylus* genus have plump tails, which function as fat storage organs and can be used to plug the entrance to underground burrows.

STICKY FINGERS

Some geckos are able, apparently miraculously, to walk upside down across ceilings and on vertical panes of glass. Their toes are coated with tiny hairs with flattened ends, which exploit the weak attractive force between molecules, enabling the geckos' feet to stick. Scientists have recently replicated this, using carbon nanotubes that they hope could eventually replace glue and even solder.

The frilled lizard can be remarkably inconspicuous. (IM)

DRAGONS

Australia is home to more than 70 species of dragon lizard (Agamidae). These diurnal lizards have rough textured skins, often ornamented with spines and crests. With an upright stance, they often perch on rocks, tree trunks or other vantage points, using their keen eyesight to spot prey, rivals, mates or danger. They pounce on prey but, if in danger, almost all scamper away quickly, some even sprinting off athletically on their hind legs, their very long, thin tails probably helping with balance. Some, able to reach speeds over 20km/h, are called 'bicycle lizards'. Males in particular, are quite brightly coloured at times. This serves primarily to indicate territory or attract mates, but may also regulate heat absorption.

Frilled lizard

The charismatic frilled lizard (*Chlamydosaurus kingii*) can grow to a metre in length. It has a frill around its neck that it can erect, rather like opening an umbrella, by gaping its mouth; those of larger males are as big as a dinner plate. Although this lizard is common throughout the savanna woodlands of northern Australia, it is rarely seen in the dry season, when it is high in trees, well camouflaged by its brown colouring, its frill folded like a cape over its shoulders.

A frilled lizard can remain in a state of energy-saving torpor for three months. In the

wet season it is active on or close to the ground, feeding on ants, termites and other invertebrates. If startled, it can run very fast on its hind legs to climb the nearest tree, sidling around the trunk to keep out of sight. "We like our lizards frilled, not grilled" read roadside signs in the Northern Territory. Fierce, late dry season fires kill a lot of frilled lizards but cooler, early dry season fires remove ground cover, usefully exposing prey without reaching the lizards' treetop retreats.

With frill erected, and gaping yellow mouth, the frilled lizard is a formidable sight. (M&PF/FLPA)

Thorny devil

The thorny devil (*Moloch horridus*) is undeniably cute, despite its off-putting scientific name – *Moloch* being a child-eating god. It is relatively small, less than 20cm in total length, and its mottled brown, red and yellow body is covered with robust spines. Tottering through the desert landscape like a malfunctioning clockwork toy, its stuttering walk and bizarre appearance are thought to camouflage it, persuading predators that it is just a windblown leaf. The large lump on its neck, resembling a head, is presented to any predator that takes a closer interest. Only small, black ants need fear this devil, which can lick up 10,000 of them at a sitting. To drink, it stands on damp sand and allows moisture to be drawn by capillary action along grooves between its scales and up into its mouth. Sadly this draws devils to bitumen roads after rain.

The thorny devil is fairly common in central Australia. (GW)

The water dragon can swim strongly, using its laterally flattened tail. (IM)

Other dragons

The water dragon (*Physignathus lesueurii*) is common around waterways along most of the east coast. Those in urban parklands can be astonishingly tame, but often the splash of one dropping into the water from a rock or overhanging branch is the first sign of their presence. In the rainforests of Queensland and New South Wales, two arboreal dragons (*Hypsilurus* spp) perch inconspicuously on the sides of trees, their variegated colours camouflaging them well. Bearded dragons (*Pogona* spp) are fairly large lizards with strong spines, those around the throat forming a 'beard', which the lizard can extend in a threat display by opening its mouth. A number of medium-sized dragons, often with prominent white dorsal stripes or lines and long tails, are common in arid and savanna regions. Some *Amphibolurus* species are commonly called 'ta-ta lizards' for their comical habit of waving their front legs.

MONITOR LIZARDS (GOANNAS)

Australia is home to 27 of approximately 50 monitor (Varanidae) species around the world. In Australia they are often referred to as goannas, a term derived from unrelated American iguanas. These lizards have tough, loose skin, often patterned with spots that may be arranged in bands. Found throughout the mainland, they are diurnal and active for much of the year, especially in the tropics. Although large ones are commonly seen, turning up as scavengers at picnic and camping grounds, some monitors are small and secretive. Like snakes, they have forked tongues that they flick out to detect the scent of food or mate. Unlike other lizards they cannot drop their tails. All monitors are carnivorous, eating everything from invertebrates, fish and birds' eggs to possums, other reptiles and carrion, thus performing a useful cleaning service. Large monitors tend to lumber slowly and confidently, trusting to their imposing size and sharp claws and teeth, but they run quickly and climb trees if threatened. They may also rear up on their hind legs,

Most monitor lizards are agile climbers. (IM)

Despite its size and striking patterns, the perentie is not commonly seen. (GW)

especially males engaged in combat. Bites from monitors become easily infected. This was thought to be due to bacteria in the lizards' mouths but recent research suggests that at least some species are mildly venomous.

The perentie (*Varanus giganteus*), sometimes growing up to 2.5m in length, is one of the world's largest lizards. It is strikingly patterned, with rows of large, pale, dark-edged spots, but hides well in the rocky areas of the arid centre and west. The sand goanna (*V. gouldii*), also known as Gould's goanna, is found virtually everywhere on the mainland – although some experts consider two or more species, or subspecies, are involved. Ranging in colour from black to light yellow, these lizards grow to about 1.5m long. They forage on the ground in dry, open habitats and shelter in burrows, staying underground in winter. Their impressive turn of speed when startled explains why this species is sometimes called 'racehorse goanna'.

The lace monitor (*V. varius*) can reach lengths of over 2m. It is found throughout much of Victoria and New South Wales and along the east coast to far north Queensland, often turning up in picnic areas. A gravid female breaks into termite mounds to lay her eggs. The termites reseal the hole, providing an ideal incubator and, when the eggs hatch, the mother returns to dig out the babies. The young are striped with blue and yellow. Mertens' water monitor (*V. mertensi*) measures up to 1m in length and it is greyish with light spots. This species frequents watercourses, where it basks on branches or rocks and often enters the water, using its laterally flattened tail both to propel itself and to herd fish. Water monitors have been seen walking along the bottom with eyes open, tongue flickering in search of prey. With nostrils high on their nose, they can breathe while mostly submerged.

Lace monitors are a common sight in woodlands. (J&CS/FLPA)

SNAKES

There are over 170 species of snake in Australia. They range from large, ornate pythons to small, worm-like blind snakes, and include a higher proportion of venomous species than anywhere else on earth. Most are hard to see, however, being shy and quick to retreat from humans. Snakes 'smell' prey by flicking out their moist forked tongue to collect scent molecules for analysis by Jacobson's organ inside the mouth. Flexible bones in the jaw and skull allow them to swallow prey larger than their heads. As energy-efficient reptiles, snakes can go for long periods – a year or more – without eating. They may ignore food if not hungry; pet snakes are sometimes eaten by live rats that have been put in their cages as food.

There are reliable reports of amethystine pythons reaching lengths over 7m. (GW)

PYTHONS

The Pythonidae are thought to have evolved in Australia and today the country is home to 13 species of these large, non-venomous snakes – about half the world's total. Pythons seize prey in their sharp, backward-facing teeth and swiftly coil their body around it. Each time the captive breathes out the snake tightens its coils, quickly suffocating its victim. Most pythons use heat-sensing pits around their mouths to locate warm-blooded animals such as birds and mammals. Females protect their eggs, coiling tightly around them and – uniquely among reptiles – shivering to create heat. These rhythmic contractions can raise the temperature by several degrees, thus accelerating development.

Carpet pythons vary greatly in colour but are always beautifully patterned. (GW)

The amethystine, or scrub, python (*Morelia amethistina kinghorni*) is Australia's longest snake, sometimes growing to more than 5m. Its camouflage patterning of yellow and brown is suffused with an iridescent, purplish sheen. This snake is fairly common in the forests of northeast Queensland. A little smaller, the carpet or diamond python (*M. spilota*) grows to 2.5m and is found over much of the mainland. It is richly patterned but varies so greatly in appearance and habitat that a number of different subspecies have been identified.

The water python (*Liasis mackloti fuscus*) frequents waterways between the Queensland coast and Broome. Phenomenal numbers (800 per km²) live in the Fogg Dam Reserve in the Northern Territory, feeding on dusky rats. When the lowlands flood they follow the rats for up to 12km to higher ground. This unpatterned python is shiny brown with a paler belly. Similar in appearance and distribution is the olive python (*L. olivaceus*). This species prefers drier habitats and may exceed 4m – large enough to take wallabies and similar-sized prey.

The black-headed python (*Aspidites melanocephalus*), with its distinctive glossy, dark head, is a snake of the tropical north, found mainly in savanna woodlands. It is related to the woma (*A. ramsayi*) of the arid interior and west. Both these species prey mainly on other reptiles and are apparently immune to snake venom. The woma enters burrows where, lacking the space to coil around its prey, it squeezes it to death against the burrow walls.

COLUBRIDS

Some snakes in the Colubridae family produce venom, but this is relatively weak and is delivered through fangs at the back of the mouth, allowing a deep bite into small prey; Australian colubrids are not considered dangerous to humans. Although, worldwide, this is the largest family of snakes, only ten species inhabit Australia and, since only one is endemic, it is likely they evolved elsewhere. They are found in warm and relatively wet habitats in the north and east.

Tree snakes

The common tree snake (*Dendrelaphis punctulata*) is often called the green tree snake, but can also be black, olive-brown, golden-yellow and bright blue. Living along northern and eastern coasts and adjacent hinterland, often near water, this slender snake grows to about 1m in length. It hunts by day, frequently on the ground, feeding mainly on lizards and frogs. If threatened, it flattens and distends its neck to expose blue skin between the scales and can climb rapidly to disappear from sight.

Common tree snakes are more likely to disappear than to face an intruder. (IM)

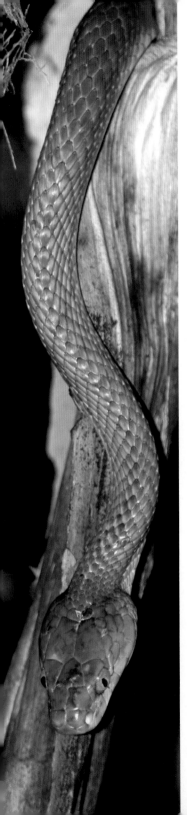

The brown tree snake (*Boiga irregularis*) lives in roughly the same areas. Most individuals are brown with irregular bands, although the northern 'night tiger' form is cream with red bands. This slender snake grows to 2m long and has a broad head with very large eyes. It is a nocturnal hunter and produces venom, but this is only of concern to birds and small mammals. If cornered – and it occasionally strays into houses – it may behave very aggressively, coiling its body into S shapes and striking repeatedly. Accidentally introduced into the Pacific island of Guam in the 1940s, this snake has been blamed for the local extinction of at least 12 bird species.

This slaty-grey snake died before it could swallow the poisonous cane toad. (GW)

Water snakes

Many colubrids are found in or around water. The slaty-grey snake (*Stegonotus cucullatus*), from northern, tropical areas, likes damp places and is most active after rain. Growing to a length of 1.3m, it forages nocturnally, often on the ground, for frogs and small mammals. The keelback, or freshwater, snake (*Tropidonophis mairii*) frequents northern waterways, readily swimming to hunt frogs, tadpoles and fish. Its ridged scales often cause it to be misidentified as the dangerous rough-scaled snake and killed – which is unfortunate, as this is one of the few

The brown tree snake has a distinctive head shape. (IM)

animals able to eat cane toads, albeit small ones, without being poisoned (see *The infernal toad*, page 127). Keelback snakes reach about 1m in length and, unusually for a snake, can sever the end of their tail if grasped by a predator. The white-bellied mangrove snake (*Fordonia leucobalia*), which reaches about 1m in length, sticks to mangroves across the tropical north coast where it feeds on crabs. Uniquely among snakes, it dismembers its prey, pinning its victim down, immobilising it with venom and then tearing off its legs. It produces live young.

ELAPIDS

Snakes in the Elapidae family have fixed, front fangs, with deep grooves, connected to venom glands. Australia is home to about 90 elapid species, representing nearly one-third of a group that contains some of the world's most feared snakes. Not all are highly dangerous but, to be on the safe side, it is best to give all snakes a wide berth. Venom is modified saliva that not only disables and kills prey but also assists in digestion, a useful property for cold-blooded creatures consuming large meals. Elapids are found throughout Australia, including in quite cool habitats; they are the only snakes found in southern Victoria and Tasmania. Most prefer to forage on the ground but they can climb, particularly to avoid flood waters. Some species, particularly in cooler areas, produce live young. Elapids are generally nocturnal, secretive, rarely seen and little known. Sea snakes are also elapids (see *Sea snakes*, page 155).

Taipans

Taipans eat only mammals and are thought to have developed particularly strong venom as a defence against animals that could cause damage if given time to fight back. The coastal taipan (*Oxyuranus scutellatus*) is a fairly plain yellowish-brown to black snake found across much of the north and northeastern coastal areas, where its search for rodents and other mammals brings it into regular contact with people. Growing up to 3m, it has very long fangs that inject copious amounts of powerful venom. When cornered, it attacks aggressively and bites repeatedly. All of these factors combine to make it one of Australia's most dangerous snakes. The inland taipan (*O. microlepidotus*) inhabits an arid zone where South Australia meets Queensland. Its venom is four times more toxic than that of its coastal cousin but this species is considered a lot less dangerous (see *Australian snakes in perspective*, page 120). The coastal taipan bites and quickly releases its prey, knowing its victim will not be able to run far. The inland taipan, however, is trapped with its prey in the latter's burrow so needs a powerful, fast-acting venom to reduce the risk of retaliation.

The coastal taipan is Australia's longest venomous snake. (GW)

AUSTRALIAN SNAKES IN PERSPECTIVE

Tour operators love to tell visitors that Australia is home to the most venomous snakes in the world. This is true. Indeed, it is also the only continent where venomous snakes (70%) outnumber non-venomous ones. However, Australian snakes are not the most *deadly*. Around the world, 50,000–100,000 people die from snakebite each year but, on average, just two of these are in Australia. There are a number of reasons. Only about 20 species are capable of killing adult humans – the others are too small or their bites are not life-threatening. Also, Australians tend to wear protective footwear and have better medical treatment – including effective anti-venom – than places such as Africa and India where the incidence of snakebite is much higher. In addition, Australian snakes are comparatively shy, retreating from confrontations with humans. No venomous snake wants to risk its life in self-defence or waste venom that could be used to kill prey.

When assessing how much danger a snake poses, it is important to consider not only the strength of its venom but also the amount it injects and how often it bites, as well as its fang size, its temperament and the likelihood of it encountering humans. An interesting example is the inland taipan, which produces the world's most toxic snake venom. One bite has the potential to kill a hundred adult humans but, living in rat burrows in remote unpopulated arid areas, this timid snake very rarely bites people. Also, it has small fangs and is sparing with venom delivered. Statistically the most dangerous venomous animal in Australia is the introduced honeybee and, apart from people, the animal responsible for most human deaths is the horse.

Brown snakes and black snakes

Brown snakes (*Pseudonaja* spp) are not always brown; individuals of the same species can vary enormously from bright orange to dull brown, with or without bands. They eat most vertebrates small enough to swallow, coiling around prey to subdue it while their venom takes effect. These snakes tend to act aggressively when provoked, rising up in S shapes and striking repeatedly (*Pseudonaja* means 'false cobra'), and are blamed for most snakebite

fatalities. The eastern, or common, brown snake (*P. textilis*) possesses the second most toxic venom in the world (the inland taipan is top). Growing to over 2m, it is widespread in eastern Australia, where its fondness for rodents brings it into contact with people, thus making it the country's most dangerous species. Nevertheless, studies have shown that more than half retreat from intruders and only 3% move towards them.

Eastern brown snakes are responsible for most of Australia's human snakebite fatalities. (GW)

The mulga snake varies from pale olive to reddish brown. (GW)

The western brown, or gwardar (*P. nuchalis*) growing to about 1.5m, inhabits most of the mainland except for eastern and southern coastal fringes.

Black snakes (*Pseudechis* spp) are not always black; the most widespread, the mulga snake (*P. australis*), is also known, confusingly, as the king brown. Growing over 2.5m, it is found across most of the mainland except for the eastern and southern coastal fringes. It feeds mainly on other snakes and is apparently immune to their venom. The red-bellied black snake (*P. porphyriacus*) is one of the most commonly seen elapids along the east coast. It likes to live near water, feeding primarily on frogs. Diurnal, and often seen basking, it is glossy black with red sides and a red or pale belly.

Tiger snake and death adders

The tiger snake (*Notechis scutatus*) favours cool moist areas and tussock grasses of the southwestern and southeastern mainland and Tasmania. Two or more species may be represented. They vary in colour from black to yellow, with or without bands, though in colder areas the majority are black, which is more effective for gaining heat while basking. Size also varies: skink-feeders on islands rarely exceed 1m, while those that feast on shearwater chicks can exceed 2m. This snake, which is dangerously venomous, is active by day and also at night in hot weather.

Male red-bellied black snakes may wrestle over mating rights. (GW)

The northern death adder can also be grey. (GW)

Death adders (*Acanthophis* spp) vary in colour but usually have irregular pale bands. Rarely reaching 1m, their fat bodies taper abruptly to a slender tail, which terminates in a thin spine. These snakes are very dangerous, as they are well camouflaged and, unlike most Australian snakes, do not retreat when disturbed. Ambush predators, they lie in the leaf-litter waggling their tail tips to attract prey, which they bite swiftly, injecting a powerful venom. With their slightly hinged fangs, death adders resemble vipers, but belong to a completely different family.

FILE SNAKES

These unusual snakes in the Acrochordidae family are entirely aquatic, feeding on fish. They have loose, baggy skin, with small, rough scales that probably help them to grasp their slippery prey. The Arafura file snake (*Acrochordus arafurae*) grows to about 2m. It is common in fresh water in the north and is a favourite food for Aboriginal people, who feel for them under the water.

SNAKE MYTHS

- It is commonly believed that pythons can interbreed with venomous species, such as brown snakes, to produce a dangerous hybrid. This is impossible, as these snakes belong to completely different families – it would be the equivalent of a dog breeding with a cat.

- Snakes do not hold their tails in their mouths to form a loop.

- It is untrue that sea snakes are more venomous than land snakes and that they can only bite a person on the webbing between their fingers.

- Tiger snakes – or any other snakes – do not chase people. They much prefer to beat a retreat and will strike only in defence.

- The death adder does not have a sting in its tail.

- Snakes do not hypnotise their prey.

AMPHIBIANS AND
FRESHWATER FISHES

The tropical white-lipped tree frog, also
known as the giant tree frog, is Australia's
largest amphibian. (GW)

FROGS

Amphibians are cold-blooded animals, like reptiles, but represent a more ancient life form that requires moisture for reproduction. The young use fish-like gills to breathe before metamorphosing into air-breathing land vertebrates. Usually this entails starting life in water but, in the dry Australian environment, some species pass through this developmental stage within their eggs, nourished by large yolks. Only the Anura order, the frogs, occurs naturally in Australia, with more than 200 species represented. Mostly nocturnal, they can be difficult to detect until the breeding season, when rains inspire an insistent clamour of eager male suitors. (Some frogs living in fast-flowing, noisy creeks wave alluringly to attract partners instead of relying on noise.)

A burrowing frog spends most of its life asleep underground. (GW)

STAYING MOIST

Although most frogs prefer wet habitats, a surprising number survive in the arid zone, where they have evolved strategies for retaining moisture. Several species, notably the water-holding frog (*Cyclorana platycephala*), burrow underground using shovel-like feet, and envelope themselves in a cocoon of shed skin that gradually accumulates in thickening layers until it looks – and functions – like a plastic bag. They may spend as long as seven years aestivating underground. Only rains heavy enough to penetrate the underground burrow bring the frog to life. Shrivelled by dehydration and fat loss, it must eat its wrapping, sit in a pool of water to absorb moisture through its skin, then feed and mate – all in quick succession. Breeding is rapid. Within a week, fully developed young may be feeding alongside their parents to build up fat for the long snooze ahead.

SPAWNING STRATEGIES

Frogs need moisture for reproduction and most lay their eggs in water. Well-oxygenated eggs develop faster on the surface, where it is warmer, so some females create foam rafts during spawning, paddling with specialised front feet to mix air into the spawn. A number of frogs lay eggs on land, often in burrows, the tadpoles remaining there until floodwaters carry them off. In some cases development is delayed until this happens.

A northern barred frog spends two years as an enormous tadpole. (GW)

Some unusual spawning strategies have evolved to meet the challenges of different environments. The tiny microhylid species from moist northern rainforests lay relatively large eggs in leaf-litter and, very unusually for frogs, care for their eggs. The embryos develop right through the tadpole stage within the egg and hatch as tiny, fully formed frogs. The female great barred frog (*Mixophyes fasciolatus*) flips her eggs on to streamside vegetation or rocks as she lays them. When they hatch, the tadpoles drop – or are washed – into the water. The tadpoles of the northern barred frog (*M. schevilli*) grow to 16cm and are Australia's largest.

Australia even has a marsupial frog (*Assa darlingtoni*), which inhabits the highland rainforests of the New South Wales–Queensland border area. Its eggs are laid on the ground and, when they hatch, the tadpoles climb into pouches on the male's hips where they develop for two months or more. The female gastric brooding frog (*Rheobatrachus silus*), now sadly extinct (see *Vanished frogs*, below), employed an even more extraordinary strategy: she swallowed her fertilised eggs and incubated them in her stomach (while she fasted). The fully formed froglets emerged from her mouth about six weeks later.

VANISHED FROGS

Frogs have been disappearing all over the world. Pollution and habitat destruction are the most obvious causes, but when the resounding frog chorus of tropical Queensland's pristine upland streams suddenly fell silent, scientists were baffled. Between 1989 and 1994 six species, most of them formerly abundant, disappeared from this habitat. Three survive in the lowlands but the others appear to have vanished altogether. A number of diseases have been identified, notably a chytrid fungus that coats frogs' skins, preventing them from absorbing water and oxygen.

The leaf green tree frog (*Litoria phyllochroa*) inhabits southeastern coastal districts. (GW)

TREE FROGS

Tree frogs tend to be very agile, leaping great distances on their long limbs and using adhesive discs on fingers and toes for a firm grip. Some are very large, but many are small and are usually well camouflaged in green and/or brown. They tend to be active at night, nestling in damp places by day when they tuck their long legs into their bodies to reduce moisture loss. To spot these frogs, try scrutinising the vegetation around water; once you've seen one you may see many.

One of the most widespread tree frogs, the common green tree frog (*Litoria caerulea*), is found northeast of a line from around Sydney to Broome. Growing to about 10cm, it varies in colour from lime to olive-green, brown or grey depending on the temperature and the colour of its surroundings. This species is a familiar resident in many homes, where the cool, damp spots it chooses for a daytime snooze include toilet bowls, showers,

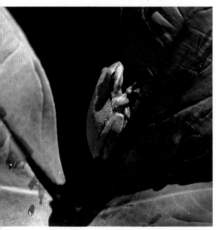
Eastern dwarf tree frog (*Litoria fallax*). (IM)

window panes, cupboards, hanging cups, shoes and mail boxes. In wet weather the male often exploits the acoustic properties of drainpipes to broadcast his call.

The white-lipped tree frog (*L. infrafrenata*) is one of the world's largest tree frogs, females growing to over 13cm. Superficially similar in appearance to the common green tree frog, it has a distinctive white stripe on the lower lip (see page 123). This species lives only in Queensland's wet tropics and coastal Cape York Peninsula, often resting in damp, domestic places. The much smaller desert, or naked, tree frog (*L. rubella*) inhabits most of the continent except for the south, living in desert and temperate areas as well as the tropics. It is pinkish brown, with relatively short limbs.

126

If looks could kill …. Sadly the cane toad's shoulder glands are very toxic. (DW)

THE INFERNAL TOAD

Brown, amphibious lumps hopping across northern lawns at night are likely to be cane toads (*Rhinella marina* – formerly *Bufo marinus*). A native of Central and South America this species is, unfortunately, an increasingly common sight in Australia. It was introduced into Queensland, near Cairns, in 1935 in the misguided hope that it would eat the beetles devouring the sugar cane. With females producing up to 30,000 eggs a season it has since spread, at an average rate of 50km a year, into New South Wales and across the Northern Territory into Western Australia. Growing up to 20cm in length, but usually 10–15cm, it is a large, solidly built amphibian, with bony ridges above the eyes, dry warty skin (frogs are moist) and bulging venom glands on the shoulders.

The story of the cane toad epitomises a biological control gone wrong. The toads both eat and compete with frogs, lizards, birds and small mammals. Worse, they are toxic. When they arrive in a new area quolls disappear, poisoned by this new prey. Goannas and snakes also decline, but eventually seem to learn to avoid them. Some animals, including ibises, keelback snakes and certain turtles, can eat cane toads, while kookaburras, water rats and crows learn to flip them over and get at their harmless innards. Unfortunately, the tadpoles are also toxic and poison aquatic life, while toadlets – which are active by day – put diurnal creatures, such as frilled lizards, at risk.

'Toad-busting' is carried out by people keen to control these destructive amphibians. Busters should be aware, however, that some native frogs look quite like toads. Also, toads should be treated humanely (they didn't ask to come to Australia) and freezing is the best way to kill them. Captured toads are sometimes used for toad racing competitions, popular with tourists.

The 'barra' is a prize catch for recreational fishers. (GW)

FRESHWATER FISHES

Australia, being a dry continent, has only about 200 species of native fish that rely on fresh water (in addition to those that penetrate the rivers from the sea). Even so, most evolved from marine species and many enter salt water at some stage in their life cycle, often because this is necessary for spawning. About 70% of species are endemic – some to just very small areas – and many are of great interest. The Queensland lungfish (*Neoceratodus forsteri*) not only supplements oxygen absorbed through its gills by inhaling air into a modified lung-like swim bladder, but is also considered to be the world's oldest surviving vertebrate. This living fossil has changed little since the break-up of Gondwana 150 million years ago and its ancestry can be traced back even further to fishes from the supercontinent of Pangaea.

BARRAMUNDI AND SARATOGA

The barramundi (*Lates calcarifer*) is sought by both fishers and feasters. Growing up to 1.8m, this silvery fish has a humped back and pointed head. It is found in northern billabongs and rivers, the adults moving into estuaries and coastal waters to spawn, and the juveniles then moving back upstream during the wet season. Males become females when they reach about 80cm long (see *Transsexual fishes*, page 130). The gulf saratoga (*Scleropages jardinii*), which grows up to 1m in length, lives only in freshwater billabongs or slow-flowing water, mainly in the vicinity of the Gulf of Carpentaria. It has an ancient lineage and may use its swim bladder as a 'lung'. Despite having a bony tongue, the female keeps fertilised eggs in her mouth until they hatch.

CODS

The Murray cod (*Maccullochella peelii*) is Australia's largest freshwater fish, growing to 1.8m and reaching a record weight of 113.5kg. Despite its almost legendary status, and great importance to Aboriginal people, populations of this once common fish have declined dramatically since European settlement. Initially it was overfished but now river degradation and human modification of its habitat, the Murray River, are taking their toll. The same fate has befallen many of Australia's other large cod and bass species.

EELS

Freshwater eels (*Anguilla* spp) inhabit lakes, streams and swamps, mainly in eastern Australia. After around 20 years in the same spot, the adults migrate to the sea and travel over 2,000km from the Australian coast to the depths of the Pacific Ocean, near Fiji or New Caledonia, to spawn and die. The larvae drift back to Australia and travel upstream, sometimes slithering over wet ground, to find a home. Large numbers of elvers can sometimes be seen below barriers, such as dams.

CATFISHES, NEEDLEFISHES AND GARFISHES

Various catfishes of the forked-tailed (Ariidae) and eel-tailed (Plotosidae) families are found in estuarine and inland waters in most parts of the continent. All have sensory barbels on their chins, which they use to find prey on the bottom, and most have sharp spines on their fins. Longtoms, or needlefishes (Belonidae), live in marine, brackish and fresh water.

Eel-tailed catfishes (*Neosilurus hyrtlii*) are named for the shape of their rear fins and tail. (GW)

These fishes have distinctive long bodies with elongated toothy jaws, marine species growing to 1.5m. They loiter near the surface, waiting to grab prey, and sometimes leap out of the water when attracted by lights. Smaller garfishes, or halfbeaks (Hemiramphidae), are superficially similar but have a shorter upper jaw.

RAINBOWFISHES AND ALLIES

Most rainbowfishes (Melanotaeniidae) live in tropical waterways, some species restricted to very small areas. Usually just 5–10cm long, they can be very numerous, swimming in shoals near the surface. Identification is difficult, as colours vary within one species. Blue-eyes (Pseudomugilidae) and hardyheads (Atherinidae) are closely related to rainbowfishes, some with similarly restricted distributions. Usually small and silvery, they also form shoals. Most hardyhead species are marine and, like fishes in this group, may have evolved from an ancestor living in Australia's ancient inland sea.

FISHES IN THE ARID ZONE

Some fishes can tolerate hot and often salty water in inland Australia. The bony bream (*Nematalosa erebi*) is one of the most common and widespread of these, forming large shoals. The Lake Eyre hardyhead (*Craterocephalus eyresii*) can

Banded rainbowfish (*Melanotaenia trifasciata*). (GW)

tolerate salt levels three times those of sea water. When numbers increase following floods, these fish are an important food for waterbirds. The spangled perch (*Leiopotherapon unicolor*) is the most widespread native, freshwater fish. Found almost everywhere on the continent, it can be very abundant. Large numbers may migrate via temporary overland flows and, when they become stranded, are sometimes thought to have mysteriously rained down.

Archerfishes can accurately anticipate where prey will fall – and are there to catch it. (AP/FLPA)

BULLROUT

The bullrout (*Notesthes robusta*), like related marine stonefishes, has venomous spines projecting from its fins. Growing to about 20cm, it is a well-camouflaged bottom-dweller that frequents coastal streams along the east coast, where it waits in ambush for prey. Unfortunately its good disguise means it is easily trodden upon, with very painful results (see *Dangers in water*, page 182).

ARCHERFISHES

Archerfishes (Toxotidae), also known as riflefishes, are so named for their ability to knock an insect off overhanging vegetation and into the water with a well-aimed spit. The fish presses its ridged tongue against the roof of its mouth and squirts water forcibly along a groove in the palate. Insects can be successfully targeted from 2–3m, and the fish has even been known, after dark, to extinguish the glowing cigarettes of streamside smokers. Archerfishes have flat, almost triangular bodies, usually with 5–7 dark blobs, or bands, on the top, and grow to about 25cm long. Groups of the seven-spot archerfish (*Toxotes chatareus*) are common in tropical freshwater streams and lakes, and mangrove-lined estuaries.

TRANSSEXUAL FISHES MEAN SIZE DOES MATTER

A number of marine and freshwater fishes change sex as they get older. One male may dominate a harem of females but, if he dies, he may be replaced by a female that becomes male. The situation is reversed in some species, where larger fishes are females that were once males. This maximises breeding potential but has implications for fishers. If only the biggest fish are taken, the sex ratios of the population may be damaged. For this reason fishers must abide not only by bag limits (restrictions on numbers taken of specific species) but also by lower and upper size limits, which vary from place to place. Ask locally for details if you plan to go fishing.

INVERTEBRATES

A golden orb-weaver spider in her massive web is a common, if daunting, sight. (IM)

Invertebrates may be spineless, but life on earth would quickly grind to a halt without them. They pollinate plants, break down dead organic matter, recycle and nourish the soil, and are fundamental links in the food chain. These mini-beasts come in a fantastic variety of shapes and sizes and, as consummate networkers, they interact with each other and with all elements of the environment in intriguing ways. While some can be annoying, a few even downright dangerous, invertebrates are rarely dull. This chapter offers a brief overview of some of the key players.

WORMS

Worms rarely excite much interest but, in southern Victoria, the giant Gippsland earthworm (*Megascolides australis*) has an entire museum devoted to it. Growing to a whopping 2m in length, this monster is thought to be one of the biggest earthworms on the planet.

Less celebrated are leeches (Hirudinea), all too commonly encountered in wet forests. Looping quickly towards any warm-blooded animal, they discreetly attach themselves, inject a coagulant to keep the blood flowing, and suck until they are full before voluntarily dropping off. Leeches are not known to carry any diseases so the worst after-effect is the messy bleeding, and itchiness as the wound heals. Insect repellent may discourage them and salt causes them to drop off.

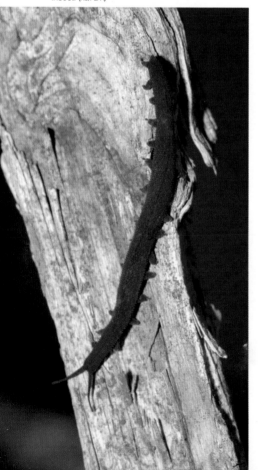

Velvet worms, with feet, are neither worm nor insect. (KS/FLPA)

More intriguing are velvet worms, strange creatures with a phylum (Onychophora) all to themselves. They have long, segmented bodies, like worms, but shed their skin like insects and have retractable claws on multiple stubby legs. Having been around for about 600 million years, they are recognised as ancestral to the arthropods (insects, spiders etc), which comprise 75% of the animal kingdom. Only a few centimetres long, velvet worms are predominantly dark blue and often beautifully patterned. Living in families under rotting logs, rocks and other moist places, they shoot out a sticky slime to enmesh prey, such as termites. Intriguingly, the male mates with his head, inserting a special headdress, complete with sperm package, into the female's genital opening.

ARACHNIDS

Arachnids are not insects. They have eight legs instead of six, a body divided into two (not three) main parts and no antennae or compound eyes. They include such groups as spiders, scorpions, ticks and mites.

The whistling spider makes a hissing sound, audible from several metres. (GW)

SPIDERS

Most spiders have venomous bites – that's how they kill prey – and some venoms also affect humans. The bites of funnelweb (*Hadronyche* and *Atrax* spp) and red-back (*Latrodectus hasselti*) spiders require urgent medical attention – anti-venom is available – but most species cause little harm and among them are a variety of interesting characters.

Huntsman spiders, like geckos, find food around human dwellings. (IM)

Burrowers and hunters

Funnelweb spiders belong to a primitive group, most of which live in burrows (some with neatly camouflaged lids). They lurk just below the entrance to spring out and ambush passing prey. The largest, the whistling, or bird-eating spiders (Theraphosidae), belong to the tarantula family and grow to the size of an adult man's hand. Other spiders are hunters. Jumping spiders (Salticidae) have extremely good eyesight, leaping more than 20 times their body length to pounce on prey. Large wolf spiders (Lycosidae) shelter in burrows by day and hunt on the ground at night. Their eyes are often reflected in torchlight. Huntsman spiders (Heteropodidae) have long legs and a habit of scaring people by rushing out from cover when disturbed. Crab, or flower, spiders (Thomisidae) can be white or coloured to blend in with flowers, but some look – and smell, like bird droppings.

The enormous golden orb-weaver spider rarely harms humans. (GW)

Web-builders

The only human-made fibre that comes close to spider silk for strength is Kevlar, used for bullet-proof vests. All spiders produce silk, using it to line burrows, wrap eggs, spin safety lines, hitch a ride on air currents or immobilise prey. Web-makers use it to target flying prey. Golden orb weavers (*Nephila* spp) create huge webs, over a metre in diameter, from a silk that shines golden in sunshine and is strong enough to entrap small birds. The female, with a body length of almost 5cm and legs to match, sits in the middle, but the tiny male keeps nervously to the edge of her web. Small silver-bright dewdrop spiders (*Argyrodes* spp) squat in these and other webs, stealing titbits. Using dense silk, the St Andrew's cross spider (*Argiope* spp) stitches a white, X-shaped cross in the middle of its web, resting with its legs aligned with the spokes. This may attract insects by reflecting UV light. Spiny spiders (*Gasteracantha* spp) have hard, often colourful bodies with six pointed spines, and are sometimes called sunburst spiders. Colonies create dense, low webs.

St Andrew's cross spider waits on its web. (GW)

TICKS AND MITES

Ticks and mites are parasites, some choosing humans as hosts. The adult paralysis tick (*Ixodes holocyclus*), from eastern coastal districts, attaches itself to mammals and injects a paralysing toxin while feeding. The effect is usually gradual. Adult humans generally notice an irritation and remove the tick in time but it is important to check thoroughly after bushwalking. The scrub mite (Trombiculid) from north Queensland heads for nooks and crannies, such as under belts, and causes a very itchy rash. Occasionally it carries scrub typhus, which can be treated with antibiotics.

SCORPIONS

About 30 species of scorpion live throughout Australia. They are mostly nocturnal, sheltering under rocks, logs and bark and in shallow burrows, though desert species build deep spiral burrows. Most are small although some can reach a length of 12cm. They seize and crush insects and spiders with powerful claws and, though they may use the powerful sting at the end of their curled tail to subdue large prey, this weapon is more often employed in defence. Australian scorpions can give a painful sting but none is considered dangerous to humans.

The redclaw is found in waterways in northern Australia. (GW)

CRUSTACEANS

Over 120 species of freshwater crayfish, also known as yabbies, are found in Australia, in streams, dams and damp burrows. The largest in the world, the Tasmanian giant freshwater crayfish (*Astacopsis gouldi*), can grow to 6kg. Six of the crustacean's ten legs end in pincers, the foremost of which can be formidable finger crushers.

Many species have just a small distribution: several mountain creeks in Queensland's wet tropics boast their own endemic spiny cray, often brightly coloured. The blue Lamington spiny cray (*Euastacus sulcatus*) sometimes wanders along rainforest tracks. A close relative in nearby waterways is bright red and white. The best known, the common yabby (*Cherax destructor*), has a tendency to destroy dams and irrigation channels with its burrows. The redclaw (*C. quadricarinatus*) is farmed for its tasty flesh.

INSECTS

Insects have a body divided into three main parts: head, thorax and abdomen. Other features include compound eyes, six legs and – in most varieties – two pairs of wings. Australia is home to an astonishing variety: about 86,000 species have so far been identified but there may be twice that number.

HUNTERS

Life is perilous at the micro level, with a multiplicity of hungry, carnivorous mini-beasts. The apparently reverent pose of the praying mantid (Mantodea), front legs held under chin, is deceptive. This voracious predator, well camouflaged in green or brown, is simply poised to pounce on passing prey. Females also feast on males during copulation, later laying their eggs inside a frothy mass that hardens to the texture of polystyrene. At ground level, larval antlions (Neuroptera) dig little pits in

The whitewater rockmaster (*Diphlebia lestoides*) enlivens eastern waterways. (DW)

sand and hide at the bottom waiting for dinner to drop in, even flicking sand grains at their victim until it stumbles within reach. Around water, dragonflies and damselflies (Odonata) pursue prey on the wing, catching it with their legs. When perched on vantage points dragonflies spread their wings but damselflies usually close theirs. The giant petaltail dragonfly (*Petalura ingentissima*) of tropical waterways has a wingspan of 16cm.

VEGETARIANS

The vegetarians are usually very discreet but if numbers build up they may seriously defoliate their surroundings. The Australian plague locust (*Chortoicetes terminifera*) can form huge swarms, hitching rides on upper-level winds to migrate, and devastating grasslands and crops. Some stick insects (Phasmatodea) can also reach plague proportions and defoliate whole forests. Normally, however, these masters of disguise are almost impossible to spot even though a few grow to 30cm in length. Females drop hard eggs to the ground where ants, mistaking them for seeds, carry them to safety underground. Most of the cockroach species (Blattodea) that infest houses are introduced but over 400 native species live unobtrusively in the bush. The giant burrowing cockroach (*Macropanesthia rhinoceros*), which grows to 7cm in length and weighs up to 20g, is the bulkiest cockroach in the world. It leads a caring family existence in underground tunnels in northern Queensland, feeding on dead leaves.

This female goliath stick insect (*Eurycnema goliath*) is larger and plumper than the male. (GW)

BUGS: TRUE SUCKERS

The term 'bug' is commonly used for all invertebrates, but true bugs (Hemiptera) are insects with special mouthparts, used for piercing and sucking up sap (eg: aphids) or blood (eg: bedbugs). Cicadas (Cicadoidea) are the largest and loudest of the group. Only the males are noisy, vibrating drum-like structures on the sides of the abdomen – sometimes at deafening volume – to attract females. When the eggs hatch in their tree-bark crevices, the nymphs drop to the ground, spending most of their lives – even years, in some species – tunnelling in the soil to feed on sap from tree

A cicada moulting for the last time emerges as a winged adult. (GW)

roots. When mature they climb up the nearest support, shed their skins (which may decorate tree trunks by the hundred), pump up their wings and fly off for a brief mating period. Children collect cicadas and many bear colourful names, such as floury baker, cherrynose and double drummer.

Some bugs exude excess sap as honeydew, attracting ants that farm and guard them. Clusters of tiny immature lerp insects (Psylloidea) create hard, protective, sugary shells on leaves, particularly those of eucalypts. Birds feed on them (see page 95) and they are a traditional snack for some Aboriginal people. Falling lerps are known as manna.

Large galls grow on desert bloodwood trees (*Corymbia opaca*) in response to secretions from a female sap-sucking coccid bug (*Cystococcus pomiformis*). Enclosed within, she gives birth first to males and

Many shield bugs emit a foul-smelling liquid if disturbed. (GW)

then to wingless females, which hang on to the tails of their brothers when they leave the gall to hitch a ride to a new branch. Here they settle down to stimulate the formation of a new gall, mating with visiting males through an air hole. Known as bush coconuts, the galls are eaten by some Aboriginal people.

Cathedral mounds may be hundreds of years old. (SM)

TERMITES: THE MASTER BUILDERS

The savanna plains of the tropical north are studded with vast, earthen mounds, some over 6m high. These architectural marvels have been cemented together, grain upon grain, by vast colonies of tiny, soft-bodied, blind builders. Termites (Isoptera) are often called 'white ants' but they are more closely related to cockroaches. Unlike ants, which (like butterflies) metamorphose abruptly into the adult form, termites mature gradually by stages. Like ants, however, they form highly organised colonies. With the help of her mate, a single queen, laying thousands of eggs a day, is responsible for producing all colony members. Most offspring are sterile workers or soldiers, but some metamorphose into sexually active, winged 'alates', which fly out on warm humid nights, to start new colonies. If these outriders survive the hungry predators that greet them as they emerge, a 'royal' pair establishes a new colony and settles down to a (long) lifetime of sexual activity and reproduction.

Termites in narrow mounds keep cooler. (SN)

Location, location

Most termite colonies are out of sight, underground or in rotting timber – only a minority of species create mounds. Used as protective fortresses and food storehouses, these are designed to regulate temperature and humidity. Some wedge-shaped mounds, known as magnetic mounds, are aligned on a north–south axis. They are built in areas that become flooded in summer, so the termites are trapped in their above-ground refuge at the hottest time of year. The mound's orientation means that the flat eastern and western sides are warmed by the morning and evening sun, but the scorching midday rays fall on the thin, upper edge. Other termites build mounds high in trees, travelling to and from the ground through sheltered runways constructed of mud. Some have mounds at the base of trees, hollowing out the trunks and branches from within and, in the process, providing valuable accommodation for many mammals, birds and reptiles (although a worrying number of hollow branches are harvested for the booming tourist trade in didgeridoos). Some parrots, kingfishers and lace monitor lizards make their nests inside mounds, while many other animals – from pythons and antechinuses to geckos and insects – reside there.

Providing a service

Termites are able to digest cellulose in wood. Although this makes them unpopular with home-owners, these diligent recyclers provide an essential service, particularly in arid areas where other invertebrates and fungi are limited. In turn, termites are a vital food source for a range of animals such as echidnas, bandicoots, bilbies, birds, reptiles and invertebrates; numbats eat nothing else. There are no roaming herds of herbivores in Australia's savanna lands but, in terms of vegetation-to-flesh conversion, a large termite mound contains as much animal tissue as a cow.

BEETLES

Beetles account for about 25% of all animal species on earth. Charles Darwin predicted that a complete catalogue would be 'sufficient to disturb the composure of an entomologist's mind', and estimates for the number of Australian species range from 30,000 to 80,000. The hard back of a beetle is actually a pair of toughened forewings. These lift up in flight, allowing the hindwings below to unfold and the beetle to buzz off. Beetles help to break down rotting wood and some are also pollinators; small weevils are the only creatures to perform this role for certain primitive plants, such as cycads, whose ability to raise the temperature of their cones may serve to attract them.

One of the largest beetle families is the scarabs (Scarabaeidae), which includes brightly coloured flower scarabs and shiny, black rhinoceros beetles. The largest of the latter are a whopping 6cm long, males sporting impressive horns that they use to topple rivals in wrestling matches over females. They make a startling hissing noise when handled. Pupating larvae of

Only male rhinoceros beetles have elongated mouthparts. (GW)

Christmas beetles emerge as large, conspicuous adults at the end of the year and, if numerous, can seriously defoliate trees. Some are brown (*Anoplognathus* spp) and others

Cockchafer beetle. (GW)

green (*Calloodes* spp). The future of the giant jewel beetle (*Julodimorpha bakewelli*) may be at risk because of alcohol. Males are attracted to discarded brown beer bottles, which, in their eyes, resemble enormous females. Clustering around these glassy impostors, their wasted wooing may prove to be the downfall of the species. Fireflies (Lampyridae) are beetles with blinking, bioluminescent rear ends. Large numbers, gathered in a tree, sometimes flash in perfect synchronicity.

FLIES

The bush fly (*Musca vetustissima*) is one of Australia's most annoying animals. Breeding in dung, swarms are attracted to moisture in eyes, mouths and noses. Other annoying flies include (female) blood-sucking mosquitoes, sandflies, biting midges and march flies. The last of these (Tabanidae) are large, stout flies, with big eyes, known elsewhere as horseflies. Glow-worms are the larvae of fungus gnats (*Arachnocampa* spp), found only in moist caves in Australia and New Zealand. They produce a bioluminescent light to attract prey, which becomes entangled in sticky threads they dangle from their lairs. Although many flies are a nuisance to us, some play a vital role as pollinators or predators of pest insects, while their larvae help break down dead organisms.

The caterpillar of the Hercules moth grows to 10cm long. (GW)

BUTTERFLIES AND MOTHS

Butterflies are moths that fly by day. Many are brightly coloured, have clubbed antennae and rest with wings held together above their bodies. Moths are generally less colourful, have feathery antennae and spread their wings at rest. There are about 22,000 species of moth and 400 butterflies in Australia.

Moths

The female Hercules moth (*Coscinocera hercules*), with a wingspan up to 27cm, is one of the world's largest. Found in north Queensland and New Guinea, it is often confused with the atlas moth (*Attacus atlas*) of southeast Asia. Both are brown with transparent 'windows' on their wings. In summer, bogong moths (*Agrotis infusa*) migrate by the million to alpine areas to escape the heat in the plains, masses often

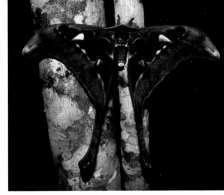

descending on Canberra *en route* and regularly invading Parliament House. Up to 17,000 per square metre cluster in caves and rock crevices, overlapping like roof tiles. Their fatty bodies are an essential food for alpine creatures, such as the mountain pygmy possum, and traditionally provided feasts for Aboriginal people. Caterpillars of the bag-shelter moth (*Ochrogaster lunifer*) live communally in silken nests, usually in or below acacia trees. Also

The male Hercules moth has long trailing tails on its wings. (GW)

known as processionary caterpillars, they sometimes travel in long head-to-tail chains, but should be avoided because their long hairs may cause severe dermatitis.

Butterflies

Two of the most beautiful butterflies live in the rainforests of north Queensland. The male Cairns birdwing (*Ornithoptera priamus*) is bright green, black and gold. The black, yellow and white female, with a wingspan over 17cm, is Australia's largest butterfly. Male and female commonly shadow each other, one flying just above the other in spectacular mating flights. Even more eye-catching is the electric blue and black Ulysses butterfly (*Papilio ulysses*). The

A male Cairns birdwing butterfly. (GW)

orchard swallowtail (*P. aegeus*), is common throughout the eastern mainland because its caterpillars – camouflaged as bird droppings – thrive on introduced citrus trees. Some butterflies migrate in winter, moving north or from uplands to the coast, hundreds and even thousands amassing in sheltered spots.

BEES, WASPS AND ANTS
Bees and wasps

Bees, wasps and ants all belong to the same order – Hymenoptera. There are over 1,500 Australian native bees, most of which lead a solitary existence. Leafcutter bees (*Megachile* spp) snip semicircular pieces out of leaves (with a preference for roses) and use them to build cells within their nests. Social bees (*Trigona* and *Austroplebeia* spp) are black, small and stingless. Aboriginal people prize the honey – which they call 'sugarbag' – stored in wax nests, hidden in cavities. They are also known as sweat bees for their habit of sipping moisture from human bodies. Unfortunately the introduced honeybee (*Apis mellifera*), now common in Australia, can damage native flowers and make them infertile.

Many wasps are also solitary. Female potter, or mud-dauber, wasps (Eumeninae) build clay pots on hard surfaces, each cell containing an egg and a paralysed caterpillar or spiders provided as fresh food for the larva when it hatches. Paper wasps (Polistinae) are to be avoided – they are ferocious protectors of their colonial nests, often built inconspicuously under leaves.

Green tree ants form chains to pull leaves together. (SM)

Ants

Australia has more species of ant than any other continent. Diversity is especially high in arid zones where they are an important – and sometimes the only – food source for reptiles such as blue-tongued skinks and thorny devils. Ants also aerate the soil and are important seed dispersers for about 1,500 plant species (see *The wattle: the national flower*, page 23).

Ants live in colonies run along similar lines to those of termites, but without a king. Bulldog or jumper ants (Myrmeciinae), some up to 3cm long, are found only in Australia and New Guinea. Able to inflict a nasty sting, they are thought to represent a primitive evolutionary link to wasps and bees. Green tree ants (*Oecophylla smaragdina*) are common in the tropics, where they create nests by pulling leaves together, forming chains with their bodies to bridge gaps. They then use their larvae as glue sticks, squeezing them to produce a sticky silk to bind the leaves fast. These ants bite vigorously when disturbed, but the pain does not last. Humans sometimes bite back; these ants have a citrus flavour. In desert areas, worker honeypot ants (*Camponotus inflatus*), known as 'repletes', are fed with honeydew, their abdomens swelling into grape-sized storage vessels to be drawn on when food is short – or raided by sweet-toothed humans.

A honeypot 'larder' is hidden below ground. (MI/FLPA)

Antplants (*Myrmecodia* spp) are epiphytic plants with swollen stems riddled with tunnels – a ready-made nest for ants, which move in and pay rent by contributing nutrients in the form of debris. About half the Lycaenid butterflies in Australia have formed an association with various ant species, which tend the caterpillars in their nests and escort them out to feed in return for an occasional drop of honeydew.

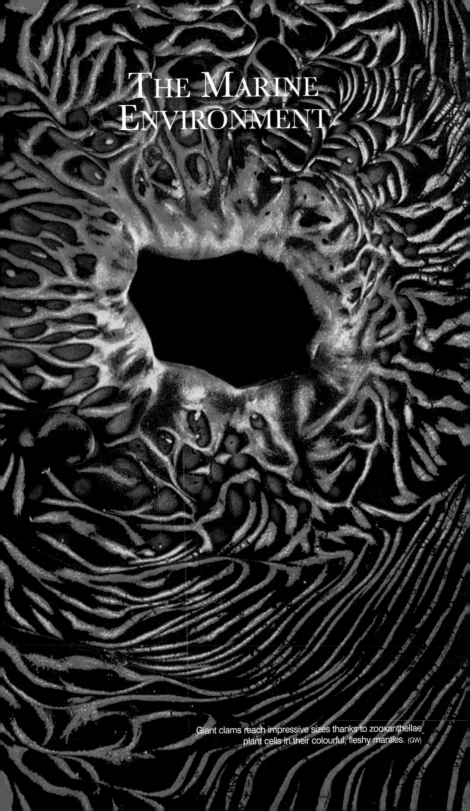

THE MARINE ENVIRONMENT

Giant clams reach impressive sizes thanks to zooxanthellae plant cells in their colourful, fleshy mantles. (GW)

Australia has over 30,000km of coastline, washed by both warm, tropical seas and icy swells from the Southern Ocean. Among the many coastal habitats are long sandy beaches, mangrove forests and rocky cliffs. Although 80% of Australians live within 50km of the sea, and love to spend time there, much of the coastline is undeveloped.

TROPICAL SEAS

Life flourishes in warm tropical waters. Dugongs and turtles graze on seagrass beds, fishes, crabs and birds shelter among mangroves and one of the most diverse, bewildering and dazzling ecosystems on the planet flourishes on reefs of coral.

CORAL REEFS

Vast coral reefs, some of which can be seen from space, are the work of innumerable little animals – coral polyps. Only hard (Scleractinian) corals create reefs and they do so with the help of tiny, algal plants, called zooxanthellae, which live within their tissues. By photosynthesising sunlight, the algae produce sugars – most of which are taken as rent by their coral landlords. Indeed, hard corals obtain about 90% of their food from zooxanthellae, only bothering to extend their tentacles at night to trap plankton. Nevertheless, this token effort provides the algae with essential nutrients. The relationship is a complex one of interdependence and, importantly, provides the corals with the materials they need to build their limestone skeletons. However, this dependence on zooxanthellae means that reef-building corals can only grow where conditions suit the plants: in warm, shallow, clear, sunlit seas.

Coral reefs flourish in clear, nutrient-poor seas. (GW)

Russell Island, one of many Great Barrier Reef islands with fringing reefs. (SN)

These requirements dictate the location of the major reefs. Rivers pouring off the Queensland coast carry with them massive loads of sediment, so the Great Barrier Reef shuns the shoreline, growing instead on those parts of the continental shelf that are beyond the reach of the sediment plumes. A boat trip is necessary to reach the best diving and snorkelling sites, although some good fringing reefs grow around islands. Vast amounts of sand swept up Australia's east coast (and creating Fraser Island) determine the southernmost limit of the Great Barrier Reef, while sediment and fresh water from New Guinea's Fly River prevent reef growth in the north. Along the arid coast of Western Australia, by contrast, the coral of Ningaloo Reef hugs the coastline for 260km, fringing reefs at times growing within a few metres of the shore. Few corals grow along Australia's northern coast because the waters are laden with silts and nutrients, disgorged by flooding rivers. Mangroves, seagrasses and filter-feeding organisms such as sponges thrive there instead.

Coral reefs are constantly being eroded and repaired, with colonies growing as individual polyps divide. The corals reproduce once a year in orgies of mass spawning, which take place sometime between October and December on the Great Barrier Reef, and about March or April on Ningaloo Reef. A few nights after the full moon, on a neap tide, they release massive numbers of eggs and sperm almost simultaneously in a spectacle that has been compared to an upside-down snowstorm or underwater firework show. Predators are overwhelmed with more food than they can consume and the surviving fertilised eggs are swept off to start new coral colonies. Special night-diving expeditions are organised to correspond with anticipated coral spawning, but this event can defy the best predictions.

CORALS AND BLEACHING

Climate change threatens coral reefs by interfering with the intricate symbiotic relationship between corals and zooxanthellae. When the water becomes too hot, the zooxanthellae begin to poison their hosts and the corals respond by spitting them out. Without their tenants, the corals lose their colour and their white skeletons become visible, glowing eerily in the ocean depths; the phenomenon is thus known as coral bleaching. If conditions improve, the corals can regain their zooxanthellae; if not, they simply starve to death. Without the coral edifice a multitude of other dependent animals are left homeless.

Soft corals actually have sharp, hard, needle-like spikes in their tissues. (GW)

CREATURES OF THE REEF

A dive or snorkel in clear waters on a coral reef is a dazzling experience. Countless generations of anonymous, tiny, coral architects, each working to its own inherited blueprint, have created a jumbled gothic edifice of bommies, tables, plates, turrets and branches. This chaotic tableau teems with life. As well as the dazzling display of reef fishes there are many creatures that will puzzle the terrestrial observer: wavering anemones, bright sponges, striped nudibranchs, fringed oysters, tiptoeing shrimps, entwining brittle stars and spreading sea fans. It takes a practised eye to unpick the fabric and make sense of its components.

Corals and jellyfishes

Although there are plants on the reef, many of the organisms with plant-like forms are actually animals. Corals themselves are cnidarians, a group that includes anemones and

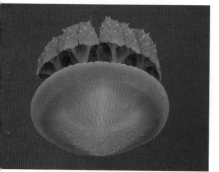

The floating jellyfish medusa develops from an attached polyp. (DJW)

jellyfishes. Crudely speaking, an anemone is an upside-down jellyfish, and a coral is a community of miniscule, identical anemones. All have tentacles loaded with stinging cells, used to trap and kill prey. Hard corals, with resident zooxanthellae gardens, usually only extend their tentacles at night.

A group of 'soft' corals (actually they are pretty tough) have their tentacles extended most of the time; lacking zooxanthellae, many are able to grow in cloudy water but do not create reefs. Jellyfishes, by contrast, are free-swimming. Some species are deadly to humans (see page 182), while others are harmless or produce just a mild,

temporary sting. Curiously, bluebottles (*Physalia* spp) are not true jellyfishes but colonies of interconnected organisms; one is the tentacles, another is the float and so on.

Starfishes and allies

Echinoderms (Echinodermata) – starfishes, sea-urchins and relatives – are a significant part of the reef community. Starfishes, some with 20 arms, spread themselves over their prey, digesting it with inverted stomachs; population explosions of the notorious, coral-consuming crown-of-thorns starfish (*Acanthaster planci*) periodically devastate large areas of the reef. Brittle stars embrace the corals with long, thin, prickly arms. Their bolder feather star cousins choose more exposed sites to sieve the water for titbits. Sea cucumbers are often found lolling on sand, ready – if annoyed – to entangle foes in a mess of white, sticky threads expelled from the anus; some species breathe through this orifice and may also host a fish that lives in the animal's gut using the anus as its front door.

Molluscs and worms

The giant clam (*Tridacna gigas*), with its metre-long shell and vividly coloured mantle, is a spectacular sight; big individuals can weigh over 200kg. This is just one of thousands of shelled mollusc species (Mollusca), ranging from dangerously venomous cone shells to file shells flashing with bioluminescence. But some molluscs have no shells. Nudibranchs (Opisthobranchia) are usually small, often outrageously colourful, slug-like animals. Bunches of gills on their backs distinguish them from marine flatworms (Platyhelminthes).

The bright colours of many nudibranchs warn predators that they are toxic. (DJW)

Christmas tree worms (*Spirobranchus giganteus*) are commonly seen on large corals. Most of the animal is concealed within a tunnel, from which it feeds by extending pairs of brightly coloured, modified gills that look like miniature pine trees or the tips of bottlebrushes. The slightest disturbance sees these swiftly withdrawn.

Crustaceans

Crustaceans (Crustacea) – crabs, rock lobsters, prawns and shrimps – are among the more recognisable invertebrates but, being popular on many menus, most keep out of sight. An exception is the banded coral shrimp (*Stenopus hispidus*), which waves its long white antennae to attract large fishes. It then clambers over them, removing parasites and old skin. Some shrimps share burrows with small fishes called gobies; the shrimp does the excavation while the sharp-eyed gobies warn of danger. Mantis shrimps (Stomatopoda) have formidable claws, which lash out with the force of a bullet and have been known to smash heavy-duty aquarium glass.

The harlequin tuskfish is a commonly seen wrasse. (GW)

Reef fishes

Fishes are everywhere on a coral reef, darting, lurking, flitting, shoaling, picking, nibbling, cruising and just hanging out. Brightly coloured parrotfishes (*Scarus* spp) scrape loudly on algae, anemonefishes (*Amphiprion* spp) weave through the tentacles of their hosts and the little cleanerfish (*Labroides dimidiatus*) grooms much larger species, even venturing into

Nemo, the clown anemonefish, can indeed be found on Australia's coral reefs. (GW)

gills and mouths to remove parasites. Slice-thin butterflyfishes (Chaetodontidae) pick at the reefs with pouted mouths, crossing paths with equally flat, colourful angelfishes (Pomacanthidae). Lionfishes (Scorpaenidae), their elongated, venomous fins like fluttering scarves, waft past groups of large-eyed squirrelfishes (Holocentridae), lurking in caves as they wait for the nightshift to start. Dense clouds of dancing fairy basslets (*Anthias* spp) – purple, gold and pink – along with blue-green chromis (*Chromis caerulea*), swarm around the corals like bees around a hive. At the other end of the scale, enormous humphead Maori wrasses (*Cheilinus undulatus*) and potato cods (*Epinephelus tukula*) wait confidently for titbits from divers at popular dive sites.

The lionfish's wavering fins may conceal it from potential prey. (GW)

A whale shark's mouth can be 1.5m wide. (DJW)

Sharks and rays

The biggest fish in the oceans, the whale shark (*Rhincodon typus*), is seen infrequently on the east coast. In winter months, however, large numbers of mostly juveniles congregate off Ningaloo Reef, supporting a thriving swim-with-whale-sharks industry. This enormous spotted shark can grow to 12m but is a harmless plankton-eater. Some other sharks occur around the reefs. The aptly named blacktip reef shark (*Carcharhinus melanopterus*), which grows to about 1.5m, is commonly seen in shallow reef flats and coastal waters. The white-tipped reef shark (*Triaenodon obesus*) can grow to 2m and is sometimes seen resting during the day; it feeds at night. Hammerhead sharks (Sphyrnidae) of various species inhabit tropical and temperate seas. The strange, flattened head – known as a cephalophoil – probably enhances their ability to detect prey.

The cowtail stingray (*Pastinachus sephen*) is named for the broad end of its tail. (DJW)

149

A large manta ray can weigh over one tonne. (DJW)

The manta ray (*Manta birostris*), the largest ray in the world, often grows to 4m and can reach 9m across. This magnificent plankton-eater 'flies' gracefully through the water and sometimes leaps out, landing with a smack. Large numbers occur around Lady Elliot Island, off the Queensland coast, and Ningaloo Reef, with a few sometimes straying south into more temperate waters. Stingrays (Dasyatidae) of over 20 species are a more common sight, sometimes lifting off from the sand as people approach.

Stilt roots anchor and support red (spider) mangroves in the open sea. (SN)

MANGROVES

Mangroves are intertidal forests found in muddy estuaries and bays, mainly on the tropical coast, although some hardy species also grow in temperate areas. These forests are made up of various plant types, from trees to ferns, all of which have evolved to cope with inundations of salt water: some species simply exclude the salt at root level; others may excrete it from glands on the leaves (where the salt can be seen, and tasted) or concentrate it in disposable leaves or bark. These plants share many characteristics, such as thick waxy leaves and sunken stomata, with sclerophyll plants that face similar water-conserving challenges in arid zones. To survive in oxygen-deficient soils, the trees produce a variety of aerial roots, an intriguing architecture that can be admired from mangrove boardwalks. Mangrove fruits and seeds must float, but those of the red mangrove (*Rhizophora stylosa*) germinate on the plant and do not drop off until they have developed a long, spear-like root that easily becomes stuck in mud.

These hugely productive forests provide food and shelter for a great variety of animals. Towers of mud, visible between the mangrove roots, belong to mud lobsters (*Thalassina squamifera*) and loud popping noises are made by equally secretive pistol shrimps (Alpheidae). More visible are the very

To breathe out of water, a mudskipper carries a supply of water in its gill chamber. (TM/FLPA)

entertaining fiddler crabs (*Uca* spp); the male has one outsized claw, which he waves to attract female attention. There are also mudskippers (Oxudercinae), amphibious fishes that are adapted for life out of water and spend their days hopping across the mud. Archerfishes (see page 130) are common and the mangroves function as a nursery for many reef fishes. Many birds are adapted to this environment and about a dozen, including the collared kingfisher (*Todiramphus chloris*), are rarely seen elsewhere. Flying-foxes often roost in mangroves and water rats visit to feed on crabs, as do estuarine crocodiles, monitor lizards and snakes.

TEMPERATE SEAS

South of the tropics, seas are colder but by no means devoid of life. Indeed, while many species in the northern seas can be found elsewhere in tropical waters, southern coasts have been isolated from other land masses for so long that a highly diverse, largely unique flora and fauna has evolved; about 85% of marine fishes in Australian temperate waters are endemic, compared with just 15% in tropical waters.

LIFE IN COOLER WATERS

Cold water diving has its devotees – with thick wet suits – and there are a host of good sites to explore in caves and around rocky reefs. Kelp forests are popular. The most spectacular of these brown algal species, giant kelp (*Macrocystis angustifolia*), grows off Victoria and Tasmania. Observant divers may be rewarded with sightings of endemic seadragons. These bizarre fishes have a head like a seahorse (*Hippocampus* spp), with an elongated snout, and a body that can only be

A male leafy seadragon carries eggs on his tail. (FB/FLPA)

described as dragon-like, with extraordinary leaf-like projections. Propelling themselves horizontally through the water, by means of transparent fins, they look just like drifting seaweed. The weedy seadragon (*Phyllopteryx taeniolatus*) grows to 45cm and is brightly coloured with reds and yellows. The smaller (35cm) leafy seadragon (*Phycodurus eques*) is more ornately camouflaged, with numerous wavering 'fronds'. Like related seahorses and pipefishes (Syngnathinae), seadragon fathers carry the fertilised eggs for about nine weeks until they hatch. Handfishes (*Brachionichthys* spp) have the unusual habit of 'walking' on pectoral and pelvic fins that resemble human hands. This family is restricted to southern Australian waters. Enormous stingrays, the size of double beds, can also be seen in shallow water. The smooth, or short-tailed, stingray (*Dasyatis brevicaudata*), one of the world's largest, grows up to 4.5m in length.

The great white shark, or white pointer (*Carcharodon carcharias*), lives in southern temperate seas between southern Queensland and northwest Western Australia. It is fairly uncommon. Juveniles feed mainly on fish but as they mature they target seals, sea-lions, dolphins, turtles and dead whales. They can grow to 6m in length and weigh up to 3,000kg.

Like all sharks, the great white is able to detect faint electrical impulses produced by living creatures. (MP/FLPA)

TEMPERATE INVERTEBRATES

Most of the invertebrates described from coral reefs have relatives in temperate waters. Many are endemic – 90% of molluscs and echinoderms, for example. Filter feeders thrive, including red sea-fans, purple sea tulips, orange anemones, pink and blue brittle stars, feather stars and sea whips. There are gardens of sponges, some reaching impressive sizes, and even corals – but no reef-building species. The giant Australian cuttlefish (*Sepia apama*), reaching 60cm in body length and 6kg in weight, is one of the world's largest cuttlefish species. It is able to change colour, flushing red to warn intruders.

MARINE MAMMALS

Over 50 species of marine mammal have been recorded from Australian waters, both tropical and temperate, although this includes rare sightings of stragglers from Antarctic waters and the deep ocean. Marine mammals evolved from terrestrial ancestors. Warm-blooded, they rely on fur and/or thick blubber to maintain their body temperature and all must surface to breathe. Cetaceans (whales and dolphins) and the dugong never need to come to land but several species can be seen from, or near, the coast. Seals and sea-lions haul themselves on to rocky shores and beaches to breed, often in noisy, conspicuous colonies.

A spyhopping humpback whale displays its white underside. (T&PG/FLPA)

WHALES AND DOLPHINS

Some whales and dolphins are permanent residents. Others visit occasionally or seasonally, usually in winter, and can be seen from coastal vantage points or visited on special whale-watching trips.

The humpback whale (*Megaptera novaeangliae*) spends summer in sub-Antarctic waters feeding on krill but moves north in winter, travelling up either east or west coast to give birth and mate in tropical waters. Over 95% of the estimated 10,000 humpback whales that once migrated up the east coast were slaughtered during the mid-20th century. Since whaling was made illegal in 1963, numbers have been recovering at the rate of about 12% a year. A humpback can grow to 18m long and has variable white markings below, bumpy tubercles on its head and extremely long pectoral fins. It is renowned for its apparently playful temperament, frequently breaching (leaping out of the water) and slapping the surface with its flippers.

White callosities (calluses) are particularly numerous on male southern right whales. (MP/FLPA)

The southern right whale (*Eubalaena australis*) is another species given to displays. It appears along the southern mainland coast between May and November, some giving birth within sight of land. Growing up to 17m, this is a rotund whale with white blotches on its dark skin and no dorsal fin. It acquired its name from whalers, who considered it the 'right' whale to hunt. Two species of minke whale visit in winter. Both are relatively small, slender whales with pale undersides and prominent dorsal fins. The larger Antarctic minke (*Balaenoptera bonaerensis*) is seen in southern waters while the dwarf minke (*B. acutorostrata*) prefers tropical waters. The latter can reach about 8m in length and has distinctive white patches at the base of its flippers. It is very curious and often approaches boats.

Dolphins are toothed whales that hunt fish and squid, unlike the larger baleen whales described above that sieve plankton from the water. Several species are commonly seen all year round in all coastal waters. The bottlenose dolphin (*Tursiops truncates*) is the most commonly sighted inshore, often interacting with humans, when accustomed to being fed, and appearing to bow-ride boats. It has a pronounced beak, with an apparently smiling mouth and is largely a uniform grey colour.

Male Australian fur seals lounge in their 'bachelor pad' off Tasmania's coast. (DW)

FUR SEALS AND SEA-LION

Fur seals and sea-lions (Otariidae) are also known as eared seals, and differ from other seals by their visible ears and ability to shuffle along using all four limbs. The male Australian fur seal (*Arctocephalus pusillus doriferus*) weighs, on average, about 290kg and is an impressive sight, with his coarse mane and massive, blubbery neck and shoulders. The female is lighter in colour and much smaller, weighing an average of 70kg. Both have pointed noses and long, backswept whiskers. These fur seals haul themselves on to rocky shores around Tasmania and adjacent mainland coastlines, and venture up to 180km offshore. Breeding takes place mainly on islands in the Bass Strait, between Tasmania and the mainland, from about October to December, when females join dominant males. Otherwise, large groups of males form crowded, noisy, smelly 'bachelor pads'. On land they hobble about on well-developed flippers but in water they are wonderfully agile, twisting and turning as they round up shoals of fish.

The New Zealand fur seal (*A. forsteri*), despite its name, is widespread in Australia and can be seen along southern and southeastern coasts, breeding on islands off South Australia, southern Tasmania and southern Western Australia. It is very similar to the Australian fur seal but weighs about half as much, has a more pointed muzzle and is said, by experts, to smell different.

The endemic Australian sea-lion (*Neophoca cinerea*) is similar in size and appearance to the fur seal but has a more rounded muzzle and generally paler colouration. Sea-lions tend not to move far from breeding colonies, mostly islands off South Australia and Western Australia. Genetically isolated populations breed at different times, with no set breeding season. Reproduction rates are low and numbers have not recovered from when they were hunted.

DUGONG

The dugong (*Dugong dugon*) is a plump, slow-moving mammal of tropical waters that is reputedly the source of the mermaid myth. Although sometimes called a sea cow, it is more closely related to elephants. Dugongs are entirely aquatic, diving to feed on seagrasses and surfacing to breathe every few minutes, sometimes even snoozing on the surface. An adult can reach 3m in length and weigh 500kg. It is grey, often scarred, with a dolphin-like fluked tail – though the lack of a dorsal fin should prevent any confusion with dolphins. Its large mouth is surrounded with sensory bristles. Dugong

Dugongs leave feeding trails as they graze on seagrasses. (MP/FLPA)

numbers are in serious decline worldwide. Although Australia is home to a large population, they are also threatened here by habitat loss, boat strikes, netting and other human activities.

MARINE REPTILES

A number of reptiles, including snakes and turtles, are found in a marine environment. Estuarine crocodiles (see page 106) also venture into tropical seas, even swimming to offshore islands.

SEA SNAKES

Sea snakes are closely related to the terrestrial elapids (see page 119) and many are dangerously venomous. Over 30 species have been seen in tropical Australian waters, some as far south as Perth and Sydney. They have flattened, paddle-like tails and other adaptations for a life spent entirely in the ocean. The olive sea snake (*Aipysurus laevis*), which grows to nearly 2m, is a naturally curious snake. It sometimes approaches divers and has an unnerving habit, for a very venomous snake, of twining around legs and

The olive sea snake often investigates divers, but is not agressive. (RD/FLPA)

dive gear. The object of its attentions can do little but suffer the inspection.

The green turtle is commonly seen by divers and snorkellers. (DJW)

SEA TURTLES

Six species of hard-shelled sea turtle (Cheloniidae) are found in Australian waters. Only the flatback turtle (*Natator depressus*) is endemic, the others often covering great distances across the world's oceans as they move between feeding and breeding grounds. Female marine turtles return to the beaches where they hatched, hauling themselves ashore at night to dig nesting pits in the sand. Here they deposit about 100 ping-pong-ball-sized eggs before covering them up. This may be repeated several times during the season. Monitor lizards and pigs raid a large proportion of nests. Surviving hatchlings emerge about 7–11 weeks later, usually at night, to run the gauntlet of crabs, birds and other predators. They instinctively aim for the brighter ocean, but artificial lights can fatally disorientate them. Cooler temperatures during development produce male hatchlings and warmer temperatures, females. Since mainland beaches tend to be warmer and island cays cooler, development and predation on mainland beaches could skew the sex ratio. There is also concern that climate change could exacerbate this.

Divers and snorkellers often come across three species of sea turtle, each with an adult carapace length of 1–1.5m. All frequent the northern coast between the region of Shark Bay, in Western Australia, and New South Wales. The largest and most widespread is the green turtle (*Chelonia mydas*). Named for the green fat around its internal organs, this species is a popular food for Indigenous people. Adults are vegetarians, browsing on algae and seagrasses. In the northern Great Barrier Reef, Raine Island (off-limits to the public) is the world's largest green turtle rookery. Over 22,000 females have been counted nesting there in one season, with 14,500 coming ashore in a single night. The loggerhead turtle (*Caretta caretta*) has a relatively large head with powerful jaws used to crush molluscs and crustaceans, although it also eats jellyfishes. It is most likely to be seen in sandy areas. The hawksbill turtle (*Eretmochelys imbricata*) has a distinctive beak-like mouth used to tear sponges and soft corals from the reefs. Green, flatback and significant numbers of loggerhead turtles nest near Bundaberg, in Queensland.

WHERE TO GO

A ghost gum clings to the cliff top in the Northern Territory's Ormiston Gorge, West MacDonnell National Park. (SM)

M ost of Australia's states and territories are comparable to, or exceed, European countries in size and each encompasses a vast array of different habitats and opportunities to observe wildlife. Altogether there are thousands of national parks and other protected areas – far too many to mention here. Instead, this chapter provides an overview of the geography of each main state and territory, with pointers to key destinations and highlights for wildlife spotting.

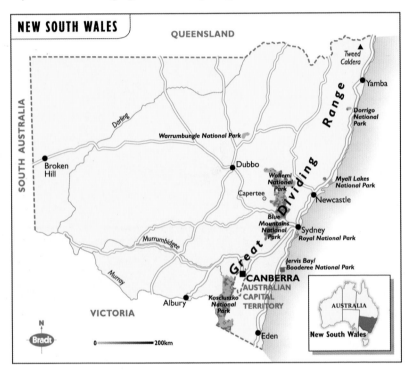

NEW SOUTH WALES

New South Wales, at 802,000km², is slightly bigger than the UK and France combined. It occupies a large portion of the southeast mainland, and surrounds the Australian Capital Territory (2,360km²). Although it is the most populous state, more than 7% of its area is protected in national parks and reserves. Most of the nearly seven million residents live near the coast. This is dotted with an interesting variety of reserves, covering beaches, wetlands, cliffs, coastal heaths and forests, though these can be very busy during the Christmas and January summer holiday seaside migration. Notable parks include **Royal National Park**, a good birdwatching spot near Sydney; **Jervis Bay/Booderee National Park**, with eastern bristlebirds (*Dasyornis brachypterus*) in the heathland and various parrots in the Botanic Gardens; **Myall Lakes National Park**, a Ramsar site, for migratory and resident waterbirds as well as macropods; and parks and reserves around **Yamba**, which preserve rare coastal rainforest and natural river systems, and offer good birding. Humpback whales migrate up the coast in winter months and, along with southern right whales and other cetaceans, come quite close to shore in places such as **Eden**, particularly during their southern migration in October and November.

Many of the state's national parks occupy the eastern slopes and plateaus of the **Great Dividing Range**. Approximately 50 reserves in northern New South Wales and southeast Queensland are included in the 370,000ha **Gondwana Rainforests of Australia World Heritage Area**. These relict patches of Australia's ancient forests include significant expanses of subtropical, warm temperate and cool temperate (Antarctic beech) rainforests. They are particularly rich on the fertile soils of the ancient shield volcanoes, notably around the massive **Tweed Caldera** in the New South Wales–Queensland border region, a diversity hotspot for frogs, snakes, birds and marsupials. **Dorrigo National Park**, with its elevated skywalk, is among the most accessible of these reserves; others are rugged wilderness areas that are most suited to long-distance hikers.

Further south, the **Greater Blue Mountains World Heritage Area** features dramatic sandstone escarpments and species-rich eucalypt forests. The Blue Mountains, just 60km west of Sydney, attract large numbers of tourists to certain spots but it is possible to get away from the crowds on a network of bushwalks. Adjacent **Wollemi National Park** is a vast wilderness area where the Wollemi pine (*Wollemia nobilis*), a 'living fossil', was discovered only in 1994. **Capertee Valley/Glen Davis** on the western side of the park is an outstanding birding area.

Sandstone escarpment, Wollemi National Park. (DW)

The Great Dividing Range reaches its highest point in the state's largest national park, **Kosciuszko National Park**. Along with nearby parks in Victoria, this protects the country's highest peaks and most of the alpine habitat (see page 34). The park has been affected by fierce bushfires but it is interesting to observe the responses of different vegetation types: seemingly dead snow gums are shooting from lignotubers at their bases; the ghostly trunks of dead alpine and mountain ashes loom over dense forests of new saplings; and mixed eucalypts on

The Australian Alps, Kosciuszko National Park. (SM)

lower slopes are sprouting from epicormic shoots along their trunks. There are eastern grey kangaroos and, at night, common wombats around Geehi Flats.

The gentler western slopes of the Great Dividing Range have been largely cleared for farming. Beyond them, the land becomes progressively drier, with the arid plains of the outback occupying about two-thirds of the state. The forested, volcanic landscape of **Warrumbungle National Park** is a haven for numerous macropods, as well as emus, parrots and many other birds. Heading further west, red and western grey kangaroos, euros and dry country birds become increasingly common.

Lord Howe Island, though 700km to the east, is part of New South Wales. The tip of an undersea volcano, it is home to numerous endemic species and harbours the world's most southerly coral reef.

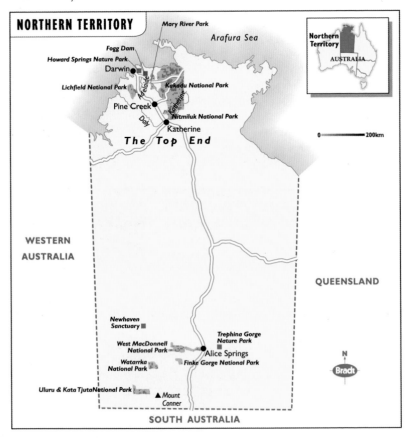

NORTHERN TERRITORY

The Northern Territory occupies a large chunk of the north and centre of the continent, most of it within the tropics. Although, at 1,349,129km², it accounts for over 17% of the land mass, with just 1% of the population it is the most sparsely populated of Australian jurisdictions. About three-quarters of the territory is arid. However, the northern quarter – the Top End, as the bit jutting out into the Arafura Sea is known – is inundated with monsoonal rainfall in the summer months.

Yellow Water, in Kakadu National Park, is a haven for wildlife. (DW)

THE TOP END

Indigenous people, who have occupied the land for at least 40,000 years, recognise six seasons in the Top End. For visitors, the most comfortable period is June and July, the cool dry time. The build-up of heat and humidity, from September to December, is intense (a time to 'go Troppo') and frequent thunderstorms herald the onset of 'The Wet'. The rain instigates a surge of wildlife activity, but heat and humidity make travel uncomfortable at this time and flooding can cut off access. Waters usually recede during April.

At 19,804km², **Kakadu National Park** is one of the largest national parks in the world. Extending 200km north–south and 100km east–west, it is similar in size to Wales or New Jersey. The variety of habitats – savanna woodland (80%), monsoon forests, rocky escarpments, floodplains, billabongs, tidal flats and mangroves – supports over 68 mammal, 120 reptile, 26 frog, 55 freshwater fish and 290 (more than one-third of Australia's total) bird species. However, its World Heritage listing was based not only on natural values; there are an estimated 5,000 rock art sites in the park, evidence of the Aboriginal people's long and continuous association with the area. The Warradjan Aboriginal Cultural Centre provides interesting information on the park's traditional owners and their intimate links with the natural world.

Kakadu can be pretty busy during the winter dry season, particularly at the best-known tourist spots, but the free guided walks and talks run by rangers at this time are worth joining. Estuarine crocodiles are plentiful and can be seen at Yellow Water, where you can join cruises, and at Cahills Crossing, where they congregate at the end of the dry season. Shyer freshwater crocodiles are seen at Twin Falls, Jim Jim Falls, Maguk and Gunlom. File snakes and northern long-necked turtles are common in billabongs, and Mertens' water monitors may be seen swimming, or basking on rocks. Massive numbers of wetland birds congregate at Yellow Water, Mamukala and Anbangbang Billabong. Woodland birds include red-tailed black-cockatoos, blue-winged kookaburras and numerous finches and honeyeaters. Agile wallabies and antilopine wallaroos are quite common in open areas, and the little-known, locally endemic, black wallaroo (*Macropus bernardus*) can sometimes be spotted on steep escarpments, particularly at Nourlangie Rock. Look out for rare rock-wallabies at Ubirr and Jim Jim Falls. Northern brown bandicoots visit campgrounds, and black and little red flying-foxes frequent monsoon forest areas. Many people come for the fishing, with barramundi a prized catch.

To the west of Kakadu, **Mary River Park** is a good birding spot, with boat trips on the Mary River and abundant crocodiles at Shady Camp. There are also 'jumping crocodile' cruises on the Adelaide River. **Fogg Dam** was created artificially in the 1950s for rice-growing but ravenous magpie geese foiled the scheme. It is now a protected haven for wetland birds – and huge numbers of water pythons, which can seen at night crossing the dam wall (see page 117). **Lichfield National Park**, about 120km southwest of

Red-tailed black-cockatoos form huge flocks in northern savanna woodlands. (IM)

Darwin, is a mini-Kakadu, with a good collection of magnetic termite mounds and good birding at Florence Falls. Closer to Darwin, the **Territory Wildlife Park** at Berry Springs showcases wildlife of the Top End and at **Howard Springs Nature Park** there are rainbow pittas (*Pitta iris*), common tree snakes, freshwater fishes and file snakes. Birders should head to McMinns Lagoon, Holmes Jungle and Palmerston sewage works, and to various reserves around Darwin. Seventy species have been recorded from the 20,000ha of mangroves around the harbour, and the Nightcliff tidal flats are a wader hotspot in September and October. Passengers on the Mandorah ferry often see dolphins and, in the heart of the city, large numbers of fish appear for hand feeding at Doctors Gully at high tide.

Nitmiluk National Park occupies nearly 300,000ha on the southern border of Kakadu. **Katherine Gorge**, complete with freshwater crocodiles, zigzags in 13 sections through the sandstone and can be explored by hired canoe, boat cruise and walking track. Numerous honeyeater species frequent the picnic ground next to a noisy black flying-fox camp. Agile wallabies are common, and there are euros as well as antilopine and black wallaroos. More black flying-foxes and birds live in the parkland bordering the river where it flows through Katherine town. Birds are also abundant in the picnic grounds of **Leliyn** (Edith Falls) section. The gorge can become very busy with tourists; quieter options are the 58km Jatbula Trail or guided canoeing trips downstream of Katherine. Hooded parrots (*Psephotus dissimilis*) can be seen around Katherine and at **Pine Creek**, to the north, where they often visit water sprinklers early in the morning.

Sunset at Kata Tjuta. (SM)

THE RED CENTRE

The Olive Pink Botanic Garden in **Alice Springs** is a good place for sorting your mulga from your mallee, learning about Aboriginal plant uses and spotting birds. The **Ilparpa Sewage Ponds** (permit and key required) support over 60 bird species, including waders, with chances of rare vagrants. The **Alice Springs Desert Park** offers an excellent introduction to the arid zone and also attracts a good variety of wild lizards and birds, the latter including painted finches (*Emblema pictum*). Euros hang out at the **Telegraph Station** with occasional red kangaroos. In the **West MacDonnell National Park** there are good populations of black-footed rock-wallabies at Simpsons Gap and Serpentine and Ormiston gorges. Birding is also good at these gorges and at Ellery Creek Big Hole. Look out for reptiles basking on walking trails in the morning. Palm Valley, in **Finke Gorge National Park**, shelters the rare red cabbage palm (*Livistona mariae*). This relict from a wetter past is more than 1,000km from the nearest similar species. Rare cycads, birds and freshwater fishes are also found here. **Newhaven Sanctuary**, a Birds Australia/Australian Wildlife Conservancy reserve, has over 160 bird species and some rare desert mammals, as well as abundant wild camels.

Most tourists visit **Uluru** (Ayers Rock) and **Kata Tjuta** (The Olgas) for the spectacular scenery, but wildlife can spring some really excellent surprises. After rain, large numbers of thorny devils may appear and you might see spinifex hopping-mice bounding around campgrounds at night. Dingoes are present, as are euros and red kangaroos. The big reds, along with perenties, are common around **Mount Conner**. In Watarrka National Park, **Kings Canyon** shelters a permanent spring with rare cycads and ferns.

QUEENSLAND

Australia's second largest state is slightly larger than Alaska and more than 2.5 times the size of France. It embraces several greatly contrasting landscapes: the reefs and islands of the Great Barrier Reef; the sparsely inhabited savanna of Cape York Peninsula; the well-watered coastal strip, with dense rainforests and major urban centres; and the arid outback, comprising savanna, mulga woodlands and sandy deserts.

ALL AT SEA

The **Great Barrier Reef** shadows the Queensland coast for 2,300km. Covering an area of 344,000km², this World Heritage Area is the world's largest coral reef system. Roughly

2,900 individual reefs harbour over 1,500 fish species and numerous invertebrates. Visiting entails quite a lengthy boat trip because a deep lagoon separates the reef from the mainland – and the sea can be rough, particularly in winter months. In general, the further you travel from land, the better the visibility and the quality of the reefs; day tours and extended live-on-board dive trips run from major centres.

The reef is dotted with about 600 continental islands – former mountain peaks now surrounded by sea – and about 300 coral cays. Many have fringing reefs and over 50 host significant seabird breeding colonies. **Hinchinbrook Island**, Australia's largest island national park, offers a challenging wilderness hike, the 32km Thorsborne Trail, for the self-sufficient. **Magnetic Island**, off Townsville, has a resident human population – along with koalas, common brushtail possums and allied rock-wallabies (*Petrogale assimilis*). South of the Great Barrier Reef, **Fraser Island** is a massive, rainforested sand island with some of the purest dingoes in Australia.

Rainforest meets the reef at Cape Tribulation, in Daintree National Park. (SN)

Humpback whales (including a pure white male known as Migaloo – 'white man') visit the reef in winter to give birth and mate in its warm, northern waters. As they migrate south again, mothers and calves congregate in **Hervey Bay**, north of Fraser Island, and can be viewed from whale-watching trips between late July and October. Closer to Brisbane, humpback whales, dugongs and bottlenose dolphins can be observed on special cruises from **Moreton Island**. In northern waters, dwarf minke whales are reliably encountered around the ribbon reefs, north of Port Douglas, in June and July.

UP THE CAPE

Cape York Peninsula is Australia's northernmost point, a triangular finger pointing across the Torres Strait (with its 270-plus islands) to New Guinea, less than 150km away. With savanna woodlands, termite mound-studded grasslands and crocodile-inhabited wetlands, this remote wilderness area has much in common with Kakadu National Park (see page 161) and is similarly inaccessible in the wet season when rivers burst their banks and spread out across the floodplains. In the dry season the Cape, particularly **Lakefield**

National Park, is an increasingly popular adventure destination. The paved surface runs out at Cooktown and travellers face some rough roads and deep river crossings; 4x4 vehicles are essential.

The Cape's diverse habitats, ranging from heathlands and woodlands to rainforest and wetlands, support a total of 509 terrestrial vertebrates. Some of these, such as the green python (*Morelia viridis*), common spotted cuscus (*Spilocuscus maculatus*), palm cockatoo (*Probosciger aterrimus*) and many other colourful birds, are also found in New Guinea – but nowhere else in Australia. Most of them are confined to the small rainforest patches of **Iron** and **McIlwraith ranges** and the northern tip around **Lockerbie Scrub**.

The rainforested slopes of Daintree National Park. (SN)

THE COASTAL STRIP

The **Wet Tropics World Heritage Area** covers a narrow coastal strip between Cooktown in the north and Townsville. This is Australia's most significant area of rainforest and, although it covers just 0.26% of the continent, is home to over 560 vertebrate animals, including 34% of Australia's mammal and 40% of its bird species, as well as 60% of the country's butterflies. **Daintree National Park**, celebrated as the place where the rainforest meets the reef (though coral next to the coast is somewhat limited), is a major tourist destination and can be very busy in the dry season. Further south, **Mission Beach** is the most likely place to spot a southern cassowary. Wildlife is particularly diverse in the cooler upland forests; eight of the 12 endemic bird species prefer altitudes above 600m. The forests of the **Atherton** and **Evelyn tablelands**, with ten species of possum and glider, and a tree-kangaroo, have one of the largest arboreal marsupial concentrations in Australia. A particular hotspot is **Mount Hypipamee National Park**, but these nocturnal tree-dwellers can be difficult to find without an experienced local guide. Lumholtz's tree-kangaroos prefer mabi forest, a type of rainforest that grows on fertile basalt soils; the best sites are on privately owned resorts. Musky rat-kangaroos are fairly common on the forest floor. **Wooroonooran National Park** occupies a vast mountainous area, which includes Queensland's two highest peaks, in the heart of the wet tropics. Although largely inaccessible, there are some good walking tracks and the **Mamu Rainforest Canopy Walkway** in the Palmerston section allows visitors to explore the treetops at eye level. **Kingfisher Park**, at Julatten, with nesting buff-breasted paradise-kingfishers in summer, is a Mecca for birdwatchers; blue-faced parrot-finches (*Erythrura trichroa*) and golden bowerbirds can be found on nearby

A male golden bowerbird, restricted to higher altitudes in the wet tropics. (IM)

Mount Lewis. Other good birding spots include **Hasties Swamp National Park** (220 species), with a large hide overlooking the wetland; **Cairns Esplanade**, for migrating shorebirds in summer; the **Tyto Wetlands** at Ingham, with abundant finches and honeyeaters; **Paluma**, north of Townsville, with a good population of Victoria's riflebirds; and **Townsville Town Common Conservation Park** (280 species).

Unusually, agile wallabies and eastern grey kangaroos visit the beach at **Cape Hillsborough National Park**, near Mackay, in the morning. An isolated patch of picturesque rainforest at **Eungella National Park** is a reliable place to see platypuses and noisy pittas, and is the northernmost limit of the regent bowerbird (*Sericulus chrysocephalus*). Tours from December to February at **Mount Etna Caves National Park**, north of Rockhampton, allow visitors to observe the nightly departure of tens of thousands of little bentwing bats. There is also a significant colony of ghost bats. East of Bundaberg, **Mon Repos Conservation Park** is a major nesting area for green, flatback and loggerhead turtles; tours run from November to March.

Confident water and bearded dragons are a common sight in **Brisbane** parklands; nearly 60 species of lizard live within 100km of the city centre, half of them within 5km. Brushtail and ringtail possums are common in roofs and gardens, while grey-headed and black flying-foxes camp around the river. Koalas are also common in suburban gardens and several hundred are protected in **Daisy Hill Conservation Park**, 25km to the south of the city.

A series of national parks protects a patchwork of vegetation types in the mountain ranges along Queensland's border with New South Wales. Several are included in the Gondwana Rainforests of Australia World Heritage Area (see page 159). **Lamington National Park** is particularly good for birding, with a chance of seeing regent

Permanent water creates an outback oasis in Carnarvon Gorge. (SM)

bowerbirds, logrunners, paradise riflebirds (*Ptiloris paradiseus*) and Albert's lyrebirds (*Menura alberti*). Red-necked pademelons are abundant, especially around the campground at Green Mountains, and land mullets and a Lamington spiny crayfish might be seen wandering along rainforest tracks. **Girraween National Park**, shared with New South Wales, is a wonderland of granite boulders inhabited by a great variety of lizards and dotted with wildflowers in spring.

OUTBACK

The vast outback stretches west from the Great Dividing Range, merging with the Simpson Desert in the southwest corner. This arid area is occasionally deluged with rain, filling wetlands and attracting tens of thousands of breeding waterbirds. Inland from Cairns, the impressive lava tubes of **Undara Volcanic National Park** support dense vine thickets and large numbers of insectivorous bats. Delightful **Cobbold Gorge** harbours plentiful freshwater crocodiles. Much further west, at **Boodjamulla National Park**, visitors can canoe along Lawn Hill Creek between towering red cliffs. This oasis in the outback is home to freshwater crocodiles, purple-crowned fairy-wrens (*Malurus coronatus*) and good numbers of great bowerbirds. Nearby **Riversleigh** is a World Heritage-listed fossil site. Heading southeast, fossilised tracks of a dinosaur stampede (used as a model for scenes in the movie, *Jurassic Park*) are preserved at **Lark Quarry Conservation Park**. Another outback oasis, **Carnarvon Gorge**, has white cliffs, mossy gorges and numerous echidnas, macropods and gliders.

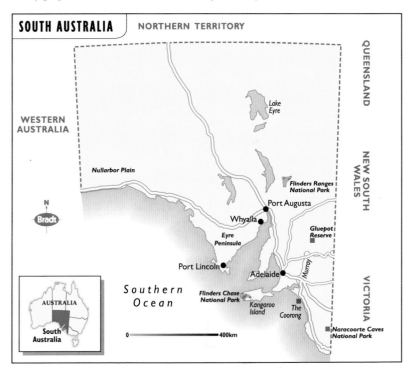

SOUTH AUSTRALIA

South Australia is the driest state, including within its boundaries Lake Eyre and parts of the Strzelecki, Simpson and Great Victoria deserts, and the vast, arid Nullarbor Plain. Habitat clearing, the pressure of sheep and cattle, and introduced feral animals have all contributed to a drastic decline in native mammals, but the state also contains some of Australia's wildlife hotspots.

No foxes, rabbits or dingoes ever made it to **Kangaroo Island** so this remains a haven for native animals. Tammar wallabies (*Macropus eugenii*), almost extinct on the mainland, are plentiful. Koalas, brought to the island in the 1920s, are numerous, and

The Cape Barren goose, seen on Kangaroo Island, is one of the world's rarest geese. (IM)

there are good numbers of Cape Barren geese (*Cereopsis novaehollandiae*), once threatened with extinction. The island also supports an endangered subspecies of the glossy black-cockatoo (*Calyptorhynchus lathami halmaturinus*) and there are little penguin rookeries. The heath monitor lizard (*Varanus rosenbergi*), rare elsewhere in the state, is abundant here. At **Seal Bay Conservation Park** about 700 Australian sea-lions rest and breed. A large colony of New Zealand fur seals can be seen from viewing platforms in **Flinders Chase National Park**.

From **Port Lincoln**, on the tip of the Eyre Peninsula, it is possible to join cruises to see bottlenose dolphins, swim with sea-lions or farmed southern bluefin tuna (*Thunnus maccoyii*), or even go cage-diving with great white sharks. Closer to Adelaide, you can dive or snorkel among the thousands of giant Australian cuttlefish that migrate to the coast near **Whyalla** to breed between May and August. Southern right whales can be seen along the coast; some calve below cliffs at Head of Bight, in the west of the state, from May to October.

East of Adelaide, the **Coorong** is where the River Murray reaches the sea. A long, shallow, saline lagoon, running parallel to the Southern Ocean for over 100km, it has always been an important wetland for migratory and nomadic shorebirds and waterfowl – although it is now badly affected by the reduction in the river's flow. At **Naracoorte Caves National Park**, in addition to ancient fossils, you can see large numbers of

The giant Australian cuttlefish adopts flashy colours at breeding time. (FB/FLPA)

southern bentwing bats (*Miniopterus schreibersii bassanii*) in summer. **Gluepot Reserve**, run by Birds Australia in the state's southeast, is a 50,000ha area of undisturbed mallee scrub protecting 190 recorded bird species, including six that are nationally endangered.

North of Adelaide, **Flinders Ranges National Park**, particularly Brachina and Wilkawillina gorges, is a refuge for the threatened yellow-footed rock-wallaby (*Petrogale xanthopus*). The park also supports good numbers of red and western grey kangaroos and euros, as well as a variety of reptiles and inland bird species. Further north, on the very rare occasions when **Lake Eyre** fills with water, massive numbers of waterbirds, notably banded stilts and pelicans, descend to breed.

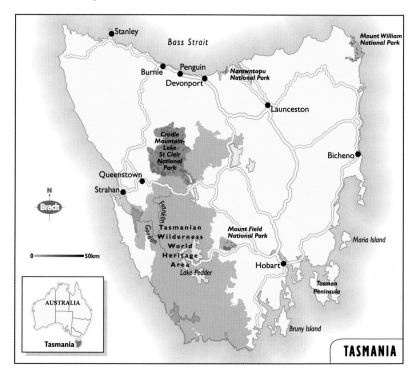

TASMANIA

Tasmania, Australia's smallest state, is a heart-shaped island 240km across the Bass Strait from the southeastern mainland. Lying in the path of cold, moisture-laden, westerly winds, known as the Roaring Forties (from latitudes 40–50°S), it can experience wild weather. Visitors should prepare for chilly, damp conditions, even in summer. Most rain falls on the exposed, mountainous southwest, a wilderness area of forests, rivers, glaciated peaks, alpine moorlands and lakes. This remote region receives an average annual precipitation of 2–3m, whereas central and eastern Tasmania – much of which has been logged and cleared for agriculture – lies in the rain shadow. The population of just half a million is concentrated along the north coast and around the capital, Hobart, in the south.

Barn Bluff in Cradle Mountain-Lake St Clair National Park. (SN)

Tasmania is the best place in Australia to see a wide variety of mammals, although sadly their abundance is reflected in the large numbers of dead animals on roadsides; special dusk-to-dawn speed limits have been imposed in places in an attempt to reduce this carnage. Separated from the mainland by rising sea levels only about 10,000 years ago, the island shares much of the former's flora and fauna, but also has over 200 endemic plants, 12 endemic birds and a number of mammals that are either endemic, or have become extinct or rare on the mainland. This is largely due to the lack of dingoes and foxes in Tasmania, although some foxes are thought to have arrived recently and visitors are asked to report any sightings.

The most commonly sighted mammals are the endemic rufous-bellied (Tasmanian) pademelon and the Tasmanian form of the red-necked wallaby, known locally as Bennett's wallaby. A rich, rufous-brown version of the common brushtail possum lives alongside a less common, grey form, more familiar from the mainland. Common wombats are very numerous in places, echidnas are often seen during the day and platypuses inhabit many waterways. The eastern grey kangaroo, known in Tasmania as

Snow gums in Cradle Mountain-Lake St Clair National Park. (SN)

the forester, occurs in large numbers in some national parks. The eastern quoll, now extinct on the mainland, is fairly common and the larger spotted-tailed quoll is sometimes encountered. The iconic Tasmanian devil can still be found, although numbers have declined drastically due to disease (see page 58). Various smaller marsupials are present but not often seen.

One-fifth of Tasmania, in the mountainous southwest, is protected in the **Tasmanian Wilderness World Heritage Area**. There are tall stands of mountain ash (known locally as swamp gum) and Australia's largest expanse of cool temperate rainforest is found in wetter situations, sheltered from fire and wind. These magical, mossy places, dominated by myrtle beech and lush tree ferns (here called manferns), cover about 10% of the state. In **Mount Field National Park** it is possible to explore all the major vegetation types, from tall eucalypt forest to alpine heathland, along just 16km of road. **Cradle Mountain-Lake St Clair National Park**, with stunning mountain and lake scenery, is a major tourist destination and can be very crowded in summer – though numerous walking tracks, including the 65km Overland Trek, allow the more self-sufficient to escape the crowds. Mammals are plentiful here; one of the best ways to see them is to drive very, very slowly and carefully along park roads at night.

The exploitation of Tasmania's natural resources, particularly in remoter regions, has led to some shocking environmental degradation: poisoned slopes around the mining town of Queenstown; rivers dammed and lakes flooded for hydro-electricity; and old-growth forests clear-felled for wood chips. Major environmental battles lost and won in Tasmania kick-started the conservation movement in Australia. The fight to flood tiny Lake Pedder for hydro-electricity was lost, but the lower **Gordon** and **Franklin rivers** – now a major tourist drawcard – were saved from a similar fate. Meanwhile the battle over old-growth forests continues.

In the north and east, impressive numbers of foresters, wombats and pademelons can be seen at dusk in **Narawntapu** and **Mount William national parks**. About 18 million short-tailed shearwaters nest in Tasmania, providing a spectacle as they return to their burrows on nightfall. Good spots to observe this are The Nut at **Stanley** in the northwest and The Neck on **Bruny Island** in the southeast, where the

Tasmanian rufous-bellied pademelons are abundant in Mount Field National Park. (DW)

shearwaters share the site with a little penguin rookery. Bruny Island is also an excellent place to find Tasmania's endemic birds and various mammals, including a white form of the red-necked (Bennett's) wallaby. Boat trips around Bruny and the **Tasman Peninsula** visit Australian and New Zealand fur seal colonies, bottlenose and common dolphins and, in winter, humpback and southern right whales. Traffic-free **Maria Island**, off the east coast, has a good variety of mammals, some reintroduced, and most of the endemic birds. At many sites around Tasmania's coast hardy divers and snorkellers can explore kelp forests, sponge gardens and underwater caves. There are more little penguin rookeries at **Bicheno**, on the east coast, and near **Devonport**, **Burnie**, **Penguin** and **Stanley** in the north. Boat trips target pelagic seabirds, such as albatrosses, particularly in winter when they move north from the freezing Antarctic.

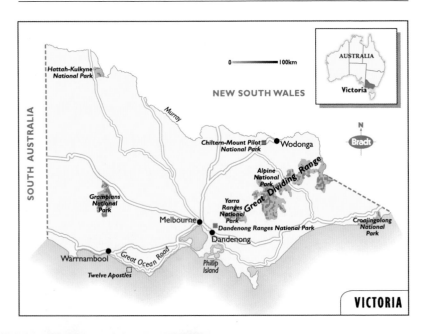

VICTORIA

VICTORIA

Victoria accounts for just 3% of Australia's land area. It is the most densely populated and most intensively farmed state – vast cleared areas can look rather bleak during droughts – but over 16% is protected within parks and reserves, including some of Australia's most spectacular forests.

The Great Dividing Range takes a westward turn in Victoria, the high country of **Alpine National Park** (646,000ha) continuing the theme of Kosciuszko National Park (see page 159), with snow gums, flowering alpine herbfields and winter skiing. The Divide ends west of Melbourne, in the sandstone escarpments of **Grampians National Park**, where forests and flowering heathlands shelter a variety of wildlife, including both eastern and western grey kangaroos. The **Yarra Valley** and **Dandenong Ranges region**, east of

Mount Bogong (1,986m) is Victoria's highest peak. (SN)

The Twelve Apostles, a collection of limestone sea stacks created, and destroyed, by erosion. (SM)

Melbourne, is home to magnificent, soaring mountain ash forests, inhabited by eight different possums and gliders, and damp gullies of myrtle beech. **Sherbrooke Forest**, in Dandenong Ranges National Park, is a popular but spectacular spot with excellent birdwatching; it is a good place to find the superb lyrebird.

Southwest of Melbourne, the **Werribee Sewage Farm** attracts over 250 bird species (permit and key required). The 254km **Great Ocean Road** and 91km Great Ocean Walk follow a dramatic coastline, with high cliffs, tall eucalypt forests, rainforest gullies and heathlands; koalas, echidnas, macropods and common wombats are fairly abundant, with yellow-bellied gliders sighted in places. The rufous bristlebird (*Dasyornis broadbenti*) is sometimes seen, particularly at the viewing area for the **Twelve Apostles** – a series of spectacular sea stacks.

Numerous **marine national parks and sanctuaries** dotted along the state's coastline encourage underwater exploration of the temperate marine environment. Southern right whales visit the coast between May and October, some calving in nurseries visible from land at **Logans Beach**, near Warrnambool. There are several large Australian fur seal colonies and on summer evenings short-tailed shearwaters and little penguins return, en masse, to coastal rookeries. If you don't mind tourist hordes you can witness the Penguin Parade on **Phillip Island**, where there is also a koala reserve.

Croajingolong National Park and adjacent parks protect nearly 200km of coastal habitat in the southeast corner of the continent, where Victoria meets New South Wales. Possums, gliders and bats are common, and the wetlands attract waders and seabirds. The elusive ground parrot (*Pezoporus wallicus*) and eastern bristlebird are among more than 300 recorded bird species.

Inland Victoria is much drier. **Chiltern-Mount Pilot National Park**, east of Wodonga, protects a remnant of once widespread box-ironwood woodland and attracts some rare honeyeaters and parrots when flowering in spring. The semi-arid northwest of Victoria is dominated by mallee. Although extensively cleared for agriculture, remaining protected areas are significant birding sites, particularly the seasonal lakes in **Hattah-Kulkyne National Park**. Emus are abundant and the malleefowl a highlight.

WESTERN AUSTRALIA

This vast state accounts for 32.9% of the Australian land mass. It covers 645,615km², and is more than ten times the size of the UK and nearly four times larger than Texas. Over 25 million hectares are protected in national parks and other reserves. With more than 10,000 vascular plants recorded, the state is a botanical treasure house and, largely isolated from the rest of the continent by deserts, a fairly large proportion of its flora and fauna is found nowhere else in Australia. Many mammals that were once widespread across the arid zone are now restricted to Western Australia and among almost 550 recorded bird species, 16 are endemic and a number are unique subspecies.

The southwest corner receives good rainfall and supports some of Australia's most magnificent tall forests. Precipitation decreases with distance from the coast, and the vegetation progresses through woodland, mallee shrubland and mulga (where rainfall is inadequate for eucalypts), to arid spinifex, saltbush and bluebush plains. The north receives monsoonal rainfall in summer and vegetation here is similar to that across the northern savannas.

THE SOUTHWEST

The southwest is one of just 34 internationally recognised terrestrial hotspots for biodiversity, and the only one listed for Australia. The relatively well-watered coastal strip is famous for its towering forests of endemic karri, tingle and jarrah eucalypts. The 86km

Karri Forest Explorer Drive winds through these forests, including **Gloucester** and **Warren national parks**, where – if you have a serious head for heights – you can climb to the top of the Gloucester Tree (60m) and the Dave Evan Bicentennial Tree (68m). The Tree Top Walk, in **Walpole-Nornalup National Park**, is a 600m-long ramp, rising to 40m, which allows visitors to walk among massive red tingle trees in the Valley of the Giants. Birdlife is good in these forests and adjacent heathlands; many of the state's endemic species can be found here and, east of Albany, at **Two Peoples Bay Nature Reserve** and **Waychinicup National Park**.

LOCAL LINGO

The local names used for mammals in Western Australia can sometimes cause confusion. Those most commonly encountered include: woylie for brush-tailed bettong (*Bettongia penicillata*); chuditch for western quoll (*Dasyurus geoffroii*); quenda for southern brown bandicoot (*Isoodon obesulus*); boodie for burrowing bettong (*Bettongia lesueur*); marl for western barred bandicoot (*Perameles bougainville*); and dalgyte for bilby (*Macrotis lagotis*).

Further inland, open eucalypt-dominated woodlands (wandoo) and shrublands (mallee) take over, with exceptionally diverse kwongan heathland (see page 34) flourishing on poor sandy soils. Approximately 20 million hectares of these habitats have been cleared, largely for agriculture, but remaining pockets of forest make for excellent wildlife spotting, especially rare nocturnal mammals. **Perup Forest**, east of Manjimup, is home to numbats, quolls, brush-tailed bettongs, tammar wallabies, western ringtail possums (*Pseudocheirus occidentalis*) and southern brown bandicoots. Many of these can also be seen further north at **Dryandra Woodland**, which is one of the best bets for spotting numbats in the wild, along with echidnas and a variety of birds. **Barna Mia**, at Dryandra, is a captive breeding centre run by the Department of Environment and Conservation (DEC), which the public can visit every second night for close encounters with some very rare animals, such as bilbies. Nearby **Toolibin Lake**, a Ramsar-listed, seasonal, freshwater wetland, has the greatest number of recorded breeding waterbird species (24) in the southwest region.

Banksias are prominent in the Kwongan heathlands and provide nectar for honey possums. (MW/FLPA)

Heading east, towards the arid Nullarbor Plain, the **Great Western Woodlands** is Australia's largest and most intact area of temperate eucalypt woodlands, shrublands and kwongan heathlands. It contains over 2,500 species of flowering plants, one-sixth of Australia's total. **Stirling Range** and **Fitzgerald River national parks** are botanical hotspots and home to several endangered mammals. Over 240 birds, including sea, shore and mallee species, have been recorded near Cocklebiddy, at the **Eyre Bird Observatory** run by Birds Australia.

WILDFLOWER SPECTACLES

Western Australia is famous for its spring wildflowers. Good rain in preceding winter months results in vast, multi-coloured carpets of blooms. These are generally at their most prolific between the months of July and November, with August–October the peak season. Enthusiasts should start in

Heathland in Western Australia festooned with flowers. (BG/FLPA)

the north of the state early in the season and gradually head towards the southwest corner. The woodlands and heathlands are particularly spectacular, while the mulga is renowned for its rich diversity of everlasting daisies. Naturally, the flowers attract large numbers of nectar-feeding birds, insects and possums.

THE MARINE ASPECT

Southern right and humpback whales can be seen in southern and western coastal waters from June to early December; humpbacks migrate all the way up the west coast. Cruises operate from Albany, Augusta, Dunsborough, Rockingham and Perth. It is also possible to see them from vantage points between **Cape Naturaliste** and **Cape Leeuwin** and, further east, from **Conspicuous Cliffs** in Walpole-Nornalup National Park and **Point Ann** in Fitzgerald River National Park, the latter a calving nursery for southern right whales. Between September and early December humpback whale mothers and calves rest in **Geographe Bay**, on their way south. Australian sea-lions and New Zealand fur seals can also be seen off the south coast, notably around Albany and Esperance, where cruises offer additional sightings of dolphins, whales in season and the western race of Cape Barren geese around the islands of **Recherche Archipelago**. Closer to Perth, sea-lions, little penguins, pelicans and seabirds can be seen in **Shoalwater Islands Marine Park**, near Rockingham, and it is possible to join tours to swim with bottlenose dolphins here and at **Bunbury** in warmer months. **Yalgorup National Park**, a coastal Ramsar site, is significant for waterbirds, including migratory shorebirds, as well as for eight frog species and thrombolites – 'living fossils' similar to stromatolites. **Rottnest Island**, west of Perth, was named by a Dutch explorer in 1696 for the number of giant 'rats'. These are, in fact, quokkas, and are numerous, tame and very cute.

BEATING THE FERALS

Sodium monofluoroacetate, a naturally occurring poison, is found in many plants in Western Australia, so animals native to the state, having evolved with it, are resistant. A synthetic version, known as 1080 ('ten eighty'), is therefore used successfully and safely to target foxes and other non-native animals that threaten the state's wildlife.

Living stromatolites in Hamelin Pool, at Shark Bay. (SM)

NORTH OF PERTH

Close to Perth, **lakes Monger, Herdsman** and **Joondalup** are good waterbird-watching sites. **Lesueur National Park**, a botanical hotspot famous for wildflower trails, has the highest number of endemic plant species in the state; 60% of those found on Mount Lesueur are different from those just 1.5km away on Mount Michaud. They support a variety of nectar-dependent animals, including 29 species of brightly coloured jewel beetle.

Thanks to the Leeuwin Current, **Jurien Bay Marine Park** contains a temperate and tropical mix, which makes for interesting diving and snorkelling. Australian sea-lions and seabirds breed here as well as on the **Abrolhos Islands**, off the coast from Geraldton. The Abrolhos Islands also have good coral reefs. Further north, at **Shark Bay World Heritage Area**, stromatolites with a 3.5-billion-year ancestry can be seen from a 200m boardwalk at Hamelin Pool. (Less impressive ones can be seen in Lake Thetis, near Cervantes.) Bottlenose dolphins come to shore at Monkey Mia to be fed by ever-increasing throngs of tourists, while of more interest to birders, perhaps, are the threatened, but very confiding, thick-billed grasswrens (*Amytornis textilis*) in the car park. Shark Bay is home to about 10% of the world's dugongs, which, in warmer months, can be seen from boat trips, along with turtles, rays, sharks and sea snakes. Nearby **Francois Peron National Park** has an impressive reptile population. Feral predators and competitors have been excluded from the Peron Peninsula, and native species on the brink of extinction have been bred in captivity and released here. Some have done better than others, but malleefowl, bilbies and brush-tailed bettongs are sometimes seen.

Ningaloo Marine Park protects Australia's largest and most accessible fringing reef system – it is possible to step off the shore and snorkel over coral and colourful fishes. Access is at **Coral Bay** but better sites are approached from **Cape Range National Park**. Swimming with whale sharks is big business at both Coral Bay and Exmouth since these huge fish regularly appear fairly close to shore between March and July. This can be an awesome experience – or an expensive disappointment because, despite the use of spotter planes, there are days when none are seen on the surface. However, there is a good chance of seeing manta rays, turtles, other sharks and, in winter months, humpback whales. In sharp contrast to the turquoise waters and white beaches, the red limestone gorges of Cape Range National Park are home to black-footed rock-wallabies, with emus, abundant euros and sometimes red kangaroos on the plains. Green, loggerhead and hawksbill turtles nest in nearby **Jurabi Coastal Park** from October to January.

The arid, rust-red landscape of the Pilbara contains not only rich iron deposits, some of the most ancient rocks on the planet and Western Australia's highest point (Mount Meharry, 1,253m), but also the stunning **Karijini** and **Millstream-Chichester national parks**. The palms, paperbarks and ferns of the deep gorges and permanent waterholes are welcome oases, both for people and wildlife, in the baked, spinifex-covered landscape. There are red kangaroos, euros, rock-wallabies, echidnas, good bird numbers and numerous reptiles, with turtles, fishes and dragonflies frequenting the water.

Boab trees (*Adansonia gregorii*) grow only in the Kimberley. (SN)

THE NORTH

The Kimberley, in Australia's remote and empty far northwest corner, is usually inundated by monsoonal and cyclonic rain in the summer; much of the country is inaccessible between about November and April. It is an area of rugged sandstone and limestone ranges, termite mounds, savanna woodlands, lush watercourses and coastal mangroves. Over 300 bird species, including 50 species of shorebird (nearly a quarter of the world's total), have been recorded in the Broome region. **Roebuck Bay** is a major gathering point for tens of thousands of migratory shorebirds, which can be observed, between September and March, at the **Broome Bird Observatory**. Also check out the **Broome Wastewater Treatment Plant** and **Derby Sewage Ponds** for birds. **Lacepede Islands Nature Reserve** is a major breeding ground for seabirds, notably lesser frigatebirds and brown boobies, as well as green and sometimes flatback turtles; DEC permits are required. At least five species of bat, including ghost bats and flying-foxes, roost along the tunnel walk at **Tunnel Creek National Park**. In the dry season, freshwater crocodiles, fishes and waterbirds congregate in pools of the shrinking Lennard River in **Windjana Gorge National Park**. The limestone ranges of **Geikie Gorge National Park** were once undersea reefs and, although cut off from the sea for millions of years and now 350km from the ocean, there are mangroves, sawfish (*Pristis microdon*) and stingrays that have gradually adapted to fresh water, as well as archerfishes, barramundi and freshwater crocodiles. Access to the riverbanks is prohibited but DEC runs boat tours. Agile wallabies, rock-wallabies and euros are fairly common. **Drysdale River Station**, off the Gibb River Road, caters for birders looking for Gouldian finches, among many others.

The Kimberley coast is a wilderness area of rocky shores, beaches, estuaries, mangroves, reefs and estuarine crocodiles, with virtually no road access. Camden Sound is a major humpback whale breeding ground. The **Kimberley Coastal Camp**, accessible only by sea or air, is renowned for birding and fishing. The famous striped sandstone domes and sheltered gorges of **Purnululu National Park**, in the Bungle Bungle Range, are home to northern nailtail wallabies, euros and over 130 bird species. Good birding spots in the **Kununurra-Wyndham area** include Mirima National Park, a mini Bungle Bungle landscape just a few kilometres from Kununurra; Lily Creek Lagoon and Lake Kununurra (waterbirds and freshie crocs); Lake Argyle; Marlgu Billabong in Parry Lagoons Nature Reserve; Emma Gorge; and The Grotto. Ten of Australia's 18 finches, including Gouldians, are found in this area.

TOP TIPS

Out bush on Tasmania's overland track. (CH/FLPA)

WHEN TO TRAVEL

You should take into account climatic conditions when planning a trip to Australia. Summer temperatures can be very high from about December to March, particularly in the arid centre, which can be blisteringly hot. The tropical north is also uncomfortably humid between about November and March, with wet season floodwaters making travel difficult. May to October is a much more comfortable time to visit the north and centre.

A visit to southern regions is less constrained by weather. Most rain falls in winter, when it can be cool on the coast and cold inland, while summers on the mainland can be very hot, with periodic heatwaves and a danger of bushfires. Spring (September and October) is a good time to visit the southern states, and Tasmania is best in summer. During the Christmas and January summer holiday period almost everywhere is very busy, particularly the coastal regions south of the tropics.

The shy albatross can be seen on pelagic trips. (IM)

Trips to the Great Barrier Reef can be very rough and quite cold in winter but June to August is the best time to see whales. Calmer waters are more common from September onwards. In the south, pelagic seabird trips are most rewarding in winter, when many Antarctic species fly north.

WHAT TO BRING

Urban centres are well supplied with all necessary provisions but 'out bush' even petrol can be limited in places. Binoculars are essential for anyone interested in observing wildlife, but it is important to be comfortable with the pair you have chosen so buy them well in advance. Cameras are a personal choice; often it is better to enjoy the moment, soak in the encounter, rather than see it through a viewfinder or screen. Good field guides (see *Further reading*, page 188) will help you to pin down identification with pertinent details of appearance, habitat, distribution and behaviour.

Other essentials include good, comfortable walking boots or shoes, broad-brimmed hat, sunglasses, high protection (30+) sunscreen, insect repellent and a large water bottle (keep it topped up). Light, loose clothing is best for hotter seasons and regions, but pack warmer layers for cooler latitudes and altitudes. Long sleeves, collars and trousers protect against the sun and insects. In arid areas a bush fly net, covering your hat and face, can save your sanity; you can buy this in Australia, but often not in remote areas when you suddenly realise you need it. In rainforests, leech socks can provide useful protection. Otherwise cover boots and socks with insect repellent or carry salt to discourage them. When bushwalking pack a small first-aid kit – with a good bandage, just in case of snakebite (see page 181).

WHAT NOT TO BRING

Australian quarantine laws are very strict. To keep pests and diseases out, everyone entering the country must declare any food, animal and plant items, including souvenirs made from these. You may be allowed to keep them, after inspection, but many are seized, so it is better to check beforehand. You must also declare such items as hiking boots and camping equipment that may have a residue of soil – but don't worry, if necessary these will be cleaned and returned. Restrictions also apply to some state borders, whether crossing by road, rail, ship or plane, so you might be wise to leave the food shopping until you arrive in a new state.

HEALTH AND SAFETY

HEAT AND FIRE

The Australian sun is very strong and you can burn quickly, even on overcast days and when swimming. When outdoors, always wear a hat, use high protection sunscreen and carry – and drink – plenty of water. When swimming, wear a shirt and use sunscreen – especially on the back of your legs when snorkelling.

Bushfires can be a serious hazard in many areas. Observe fire bans strictly, heed warnings and reconsider walks in fire-prone areas on extremely hot, dry and

Dry season fire in the savanna region. (SN)

windy days. If caught in a bushfire, do not try to outrun it, especially uphill, or cross its path. If possible, head for a deep, creek pool or a clear area (rocks or dirt). Keep low to the ground in a depression or behind rocks, and cover skin – with soil, if necessary – to protect it from dangerous radiant heat. If you are caught in a vehicle, do not drive through dense smoke. Close the windows, crouch down and cover yourself, preferably with a woollen blanket, but if the vehicle starts to burn, leave and head for the nearest burnt-out area.

DANGERS ON LAND

Organise bushwalks sensibly and inform a responsible person of your plans. Do not leave the track; there is a lot of country to get lost in. Avoid camping under eucalypt trees, which often drop branches. No land animals prey on people but some defend themselves with effective bites and stings. Although Australia's venomous snakes are infamous, fatality rates are very low (see *Australian snakes in perspective*, page 120). For protection, you should always wear closed shoes and, ideally, long trousers. In the event of a bite, it is most important to prevent the venom from moving into the general circulation so the victim should move as little as possible. Apply a firm pressure bandage – as for a sprain – over the bite site, wrapping towards the trunk, and do not remove it. Do not use a tourniquet, suck or cut the wound, or wash it – traces of venom help with identification. Do not try to kill the snake – or any snake – as that is when most people get bitten. Seek urgent medical assistance.

Most spiders have a venomous bite but, like snakes, prefer to retreat and not waste venom on non-prey animals. Some can cause fatalities, as can the paralysis tick (see page 134), but thanks to medical treatment these are rare. Dangers usually come from less

Do not touch! The stinging tree has heart-shaped, serrated leaves and pink, raspberry-like fruit. (DW)

obvious sources. Stinging trees (*Dendrocnide* spp), found in east coast rainforests, are covered with hairs that inject a powerful toxin causing intense, long-lasting pain. Learn to recognise this plant – and do not wander off tracks. There is no malaria in Australia but mosquitoes can carry other diseases, so apply insect repellent and wear long sleeves and trousers, especially in wetland or forest environments.

Spot the croc. (DW)

DANGERS IN THE WATER

Crocodiles are a serious danger in northern waters, both fresh and salt (see page 107), and tropical coastal waters are also home to some almost invisible, but extremely dangerous, stinging jellyfishes. Box jellyfish (*Chironex fleckeri*), known as 'stingers', are present close to the coast between October and May. Do not swim in coastal tropical waters in summer outside special stinger nets on popular beaches – although small irukandji jellyfish (*Carukia barnesi*) can slip through these. If someone is stung, douse the site with vinegar, seek urgent medical assistance and be prepared to use artificial respiration.

A number of other marine creatures are venomous, with cone shell (Conidae) stings and blue-ringed octopus (*Hapalochlaena* spp) bites being potentially fatal. To avoid unpleasant surprises, it is best to avoid touching anything underwater. Limbs affected by stingray, crown-of-thorns starfish, sea urchin, stonefish and freshwater bullrout stings should be immersed in hot, but not scalding, water; this both relieves pain and often destroys the venom. Many beaches are protected with shark nets but take local advice on where to swim – also in relation to dangerous rip currents. Avoid wading or swimming at dusk and never carry bleeding fishes underwater. Reef sharks are unlikely to bother you but a more unexpected threat comes from the titan triggerfish (*Balistoides viridescens*), which, in the summer breeding season, may suddenly charge and bite divers who come near its nest. Never eat fishes, such as toadfishes, which inflate their bodies when provoked. These contain a deadly poison.

A BIT OF PERSPECTIVE

In Australia, in an average year, 1.2 people are killed by sharks (compared with 100 million sharks killed by humans, worldwide), 1.8 by crocodiles, 2.5 by bee and wasp stings, 2.6 by snake and lizard bites, 18.3 by falling off ladders and over 1,500 in road accidents.

DRIVING

Much is made of Australia's dangerous wildlife but – as in any part of the world – driving is the most hazardous thing you will do. You should avoid driving on outback roads from late afternoon to morning. As carcasses at the roadside testify, macropods have absolutely no road sense and are likely to bound across your path; Australian vehicles are commonly equipped with 'bull-bars' or 'roo-bars' to minimise damage. If an animal does appear on a collision course, do not swerve – this is one of the main causes of single vehicle roll-overs, especially in 4x4 vehicles and campervans. You should be aware, whether driving or bushwalking, that in the tropics it gets dark very quickly, within half an hour of sunset, and that last light can be as early as 18.00 in the winter dry season and not much later in summer. Check insurance policies on hired vehicles before planning trips on unsealed roads, which are common in remote areas.

River crossings can be hazardous, particularly after heavy rain. Before attempting to ford in a 4x4

Roadside casualty – an endangered Lumholtz's tree-kangaroo. (SM)

it is advisable, if safe, to walk across first – but not in crocodile country. If the water depth is above thigh level, or if the rate of flow prevents a safe crossing, do not drive across. Also beware of submerged debris such as trees and branches. Contact the state Royal Automobile Club (RAC) and/or Bureau of Meteorology for travel and weather advice.

Driving in arid regions also has its hazards. Pot-holes filled with powdery sand 'bulldust' can be deeper than they seem. If you are intending to head into remote areas, seek local advice on road conditions and register your plans with local police or a responsible person (and make sure to let them know when you have completed your trip). Always carry plenty of fuel, water and spares. Consider taking a satellite phone with you, as many remote areas do not have mobile phone coverage, as well as a GPS, if you know how to use it. If you do break down, remain near your vehicle and wait for help to arrive. In Australia, dial 000 for Emergency but if having difficulty on a mobile phone try 112.

SPOTTING WILDLIFE

Do not underestimate the size of Australia and don't try to see everything in one short trip. You can spend a lot of precious time driving huge distances. Instead, pick a limited number of destinations, take your time and be observant. Plan according to season (see *When to travel*, page 180) but listen for news of unusual events. Rain in the arid zone will stimulate a blossoming of wildflowers. Unusual rainfall can fill inland wetlands that have been dry for years, such as Lake Eyre, attracting massive numbers of breeding birds. New growth after bushfires will attract herbivores.

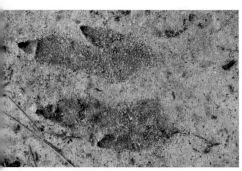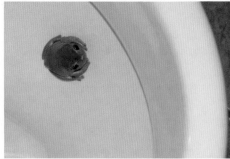

Look out for kangaroo tracks in the sand (left, SM) and for wildlife in unexpected places (right, DW).

LOOK CLOSER

Many animals are secretive and elusive. By walking slowly and quietly through the bush you increase your chance of taking them by surprise – perhaps a sunning perentie, an echidna digging for ants or a lyrebird scratching in the leaf-litter. Take your time and wait a while in promising locations. Stopping by a creek you might notice a colourful crayfish edging out from under a rock, a surfacing platypus, a water dragon sitting motionless on a branch or a kingfisher flitting downstream. Standing in the forest you will become aware of birds feeding in the canopy or chasing through the undergrowth, and you might hear the telltale rustle of a foraging wallaby. Sitting discreetly near a desert waterhole you can watch thirsty birds arriving to drink.

Learn to recognise habitats and what to expect there; the ecotone zone where one habitat meets another is often worth exploring. You can frequently get closer to an animal in a vehicle. If on foot, approach at an angle as if walking past. 'Pishing' and squeaking sounds may attract curious birds. Look for tracks, scats, diggings, scratchings and other signs of passing visitors or nocturnal dramas. Bandicoots dig distinctive cone-shaped pits; wombats produce characteristic, cube-shaped droppings; turned leaf-litter and churned ground can indicate the presence of lyrebirds, brush-turkeys … or pigs; strewn feathers may be the work of a quoll or raptor (or feral cat); and a striped possum might have shredded that rotting log.

DAY AND NIGHT

Time of day is also important. Birds are generally more active at dawn and dusk but in colder areas, such as Tasmania, they might be busy all day. Reptiles often sun themselves in the earlier part of the day – or on warm roads after dark. Birds and other animals visit waterholes to drink in the morning.

Most mammals are nocturnal. Some species may be visible by day: mobs of roos shelter under trees, koalas snooze on branches, flying-foxes gather in noisy camps and dull weather can bring out creatures such as platypuses. For others, however, dusk is generally the best time to look. Rock-wallabies emerge to warm themselves in the last light, swarms of insectivorous bats flow from cave mouths, flying-foxes stream out across the evening sky, and gliders and possums emerge from their holes (you can stake out promising hollows).

Camping is a good way to encounter nocturnal animals, some of which might try to join you (though please do not feed them). A good spotting method, in mammal-rich places such as Tasmania, is to drive extremely slowly (5–10km/h) and carefully – macropods, brushtail possums, quolls, wombats and even Tasmanian devils may appear in the headlights. Alternatively, take a walk on a moonless night (mammals hide away from a full moon) with a spotlight – no more than 30W. Hold it close to your head so you can look along the beam and catch sight of eye-shine – a bright reflection that sometimes varies in colour according to species – but when you do spot an animal, move the light away from its head and cover the lens

Most mammals, such as this spotted-tailed quoll, are usually seen only at night. (DH/FLPA)

with a red filter (cellophane will work) to reduce stress. If you are quiet, and the animal not dazzled, it is likely to ignore you. Use your binoculars, don't shine the light on roosting or nesting birds (including penguins) and carry a torch in case the spotlight battery runs out. A head torch helps, as you can keep it trained on the animal while your hands are free to hold camera or binoculars. Frogs can be difficult to find, in spite of their loud calls, but if two or three people shine torches at the spot they think the noise is coming from, you may spot them near where the beams intersect.

GUIDES AND TOURS

You may like to travel at your own pace and make your own discoveries, or you may prefer, occasionally, to rely on a guide with local knowledge. Many tours are touted as 'eco-adventures' but the main focus may be on landscape, waterfalls and having a good time with guides who might not like the truth to get in the way of a colourful story ('bus-driver dreaming'). It is worth checking for tours with Ecotourism Australia accreditation and, across the north, the Savannah Guides organisation – a network of well-trained and knowledgeable professionals. Specialised bird tours and localised spotlighting trips, particularly useful for those elusive arboreal mammals, are usually run by people who know when and where to look for target species. In many places it is possible to join tours conducted by Aboriginal guides who provide a different, and fascinating, perspective on their 'country', its wildlife and their relation to it. Birders might like to join Bird Observation and Conservation Australia and link up with local enthusiasts who are often glad to show off their patch. Keep an eye out in tourism centres for locally produced guides to birds and other wildlife, and ask in national park offices for species lists.

NATIONAL PARKS AND SANCTUARIES

Most national parks are administered by state authorities, but some, such as Kakadu and Uluru-Kata Tjuta, are under federal control. Entry fees are charged in some states and it is often (but not always) worth buying a state season pass. Check national park offices and websites for detailed park information as well as for closures, which can be unexpected due

Dolphin feeding at Monkey Mia is now strictly controlled by rangers. (SM)

to weather conditions, and look out for ranger-guided walks and talks, usually in school holidays. There are also forestry, water and local council reserves, as well as areas protected by non-government organisations, such as Australian Wildlife Conservancy, Australian Bush Heritage Fund and Birds Australia, some of them open to the public. Aboriginal reserves usually have strict entry restrictions.

All the capital cities, and many smaller towns, have excellent botanic gardens, which are a haven for local birds and other wildlife. In places, heavily fenced, predator-free, sanctuaries – both publicly and privately owned – have been set up as captive breeding centres for critically endangered animals. Some of these are open to the public, providing an opportunity to see very rare animals. Similarly, most zoos and wildlife parks have good native animal sections, often with nocturnal houses and walk-through aviaries. These animals are sometimes part of a captive breeding programme, or may be orphaned or injured creatures that cannot be released. While this is not the same as seeing the animals in the wild, it is often your only opportunity to see small, secretive and rare species and may enhance your chances of recognising an animal later. When laid out well, showcasing the local environment, these places can be a magnet for local free-living wildlife, especially birds and reptiles.

MINIMAL IMPACT

As with all protected areas worldwide, please stay on tracks to prevent erosion, remove rubbish, abide by fire bans and do not bring domestic animals into parks. Please don't feed wild animals. They can become dependent on artificial food, develop illnesses from it and become aggressive and/or vulnerable to attack from dogs and other predators. Also avoid leaving food where it might exacerbate the problem.

Phythopthora is a soil organism (related to potato blight) responsible for drastic forest dieback in many parts of Australia. It can be spread via soil clinging to boots, vehicles and camping gear, so it is a good idea to clean off soil between trips. This also helps to minimise the spread of weed seeds.

WILDLIFE PHOTOGRAPHY

The digital revolution has made wildlife photography easier for the amateur. Many of today's compact 'point and shoot' cameras have inbuilt zoom lenses that offer magnification similar to telephoto lenses. Use the 'optical zoom' element (avoiding the oft-hyped but low-quality 'digital zoom'), choose the 'action' setting (often depicted by a running man), and you should achieve some reasonable images.

For really good results, however, it pays to invest in an SLR camera and a telephoto lens. The longer the lens, the closer you can get to an animal without disturbing it; 200mm is adequate, but 400mm ideal. A zoom lens (eg: 70–300 mm) offers more compositional flexibility, but generally lacks the sharpness of a fixed (prime) lens.

While longer lenses are a must, they tend to be hefty. The heavier a lens, and the closer you zoom in, the greater the prospect of camera shake ruining the shot. There are several ways around this. A lens with inbuilt image stabilisation – although pricy – helps, particularly in low light. If shooting from a stationary vehicle, use the window frame as a support, buffered by a beanbag (a bag of oats or bunched-up clothing will do). A tripod is useful for stationary subjects, or when in a hide, but it can prove clumsy when stalking wildlife; tree trunks and limbs often make good alternatives.

Sound technique is also essential. Wait patiently for an animal to get used to your presence. Shoot a moving animal on a fast shutter speed to freeze the action. For a close creature, increase the depth of field to bring its entire body into focus. Getting down low to an animal's level can create a more intimate portrait.

Australian light can be harsh, and in very bright situations it often helps to stop down a little to prevent white and light colours being washed out – later adjusting the light balance on your computer. Try to avoid snapping subjects with the light behind them; walk around, at a distance, to find a better position. Early morning and late afternoon, when the shadows are longer, can offer the best light conditions. Heat haze can also be a problem, particularly later in the day and if there is a cool breeze.

Look after your gear. In potentially wet situations, such as the tropics and on boats, make sure you have a backpack, or sealable (snap-lock) plastic bags to protect it. A folding umbrella or lightweight waterproof cape is also useful. Equipment may not be available in remote areas so make sure you carry spare batteries, chargers, memory cards and so on. If camping, you can't rely on access to mains power for recharging; car adapters are a good alternative. Always back up your photos on an external hard drive or disk, and keep them in a safe place.

Wait patiently for an animal to get used to your presence! (MIW/FLPA)

FURTHER READING

Many books – field guides as well as hefty reference books – have been written about various aspects of Australian wildlife. For this list, I have selected those books that I find most useful in the field and those that I found most helpful when writing this book. I have also added some informative websites.

GUIDES
MAMMALS

A Field Guide to the Mammals of Australia. Peter Menkhorst and Frank Knight. Oxford University Press (2004). A handy-sized guide with comprehensive descriptions and distribution maps facing good illustrations of all species.

The Mammals of Australia (3rd edition). Steve Van Dyck and Ronald Strahan (eds). Reed New Holland (2008). A tome, not a field guide, but the most comprehensive guide to Australia's mammals. Full detail on identification and behaviour for each species.

Tracks, Scats and other Traces: A Field Guide to Australian Mammals. Barbara Triggs. Oxford University Press (2008). An excellent identification guide to clues left by mammals, including footprints, scats, diggings and skulls. Ideal for the wildlife detective.

BIRDS

The Field Guide to the Birds of Australia (8th edition). Graham Pizzey and Frank Knight. HarperCollins Publishers (2007). The best guide to Australia's birds, though a bit heavy (over 1kg) for use in the field. Accurate illustrations and good detail on distribution, 'similar species' and other information.

The Slater Field Guide to Australian Birds (2nd edition). Peter Slater, Pat Slater and Raoul Slater. New Holland (2009). This much lighter book is the best for use in the field, with texts and maps facing good colour illustrations.

Field Guide to the Birds of Australia (7th edition). Ken Simpson and Nicolas Day. Viking Penguin (2004). Nearly as heavy as the Pizzey but with briefer species notes. Good illustrations, with pointers to key identification markers, and maps, plus long section on habitats, behaviour and so on.

Birding Australia Directory. Lloyd Nielsen. Published Lloyd Nielsen (2009). A spiral-bound, self-published guide that details Australia's best birding sites and includes tips on when to visit, local contacts, accommodation and more. One edition for Australian birders and an international edition aimed at first-time visitors. Available (along with some regional guides) online: www.birdingaustralia.com.au.

The Complete Guide to Finding the Birds of Australia (2nd edition). Richard Thomas, Alan McBride and David Andrew. CSIRO Publishing (2010). A revised and updated version of an excellent guide, listing good birding sites across the country.

OTHER WILDLIFE

A Complete Guide to Reptiles of Australia (2nd edition). Steve Wilson and Gerry Swan. New Holland (2008). A comprehensive guide with clear photos of more than 800 species.

Includes an introduction to each family and genus, plus concise descriptions and distribution maps for each species.

Field Guide to the Frogs of Australia. Michael J Tyler and Frank Knight. CSIRO Publishing (2009). A fully illustrated guide to all the known frogs of Australia, with concise accounts of 227 species within the five main families.

Field Guide to the Freshwater Fishes of Australia. G R Allen, S H Midgley and M Allen. Western Australian Museum (2002). A comprehensive guide to native freshwater fishes, including the marginal estuarine-freshwater fishes and introduced families, plus an overview of the drainage divisions.

A Field Guide to Insects in Australia (3rd edition). Paul Zborowski and Ross Storey. New Holland (2010). It's a tall order to cover all Australian insects in one small book but this provides an excellent overview of main orders and families, with useful photographs.

Australian Tropical Butterflies. Peter Valentine, Clifford Frith and Dawn Frith. Frith & Frith Books (1991). This handy guide covers many of the most commonly seen butterflies from Australia's north.

The Complete Field Guide to Butterflies of Australia. Michael J Braby CSIRO Publishing (2004). This somewhat weightier book covers all Australian species.

Australian Wildlife: Roadkill. Len Zell. Wild Discovery Guides (2006). Sadly, a useful book for travellers in Australia.

The Geology of Australia (2nd edition). David Johnson. Cambridge University Press (2009). An excellent introduction to the rocks that underpin life in Australia.

MARINE

Indo-Pacific Coral Reef Field Guide. Dr Gerald R Allen and Roger Steene. Tropical Reef Research (2007). This excellent, concise guide covers fishes and plants, plus corals and other invertebrate groups, with good photographs and short chapter introductions. Most species are found in Australian tropical waters.

Tropical Pacific Invertebrates. Patrick L Colin and Charles Arneson. The Coral Reef Research Foundation (1995). This larger book covers just the invertebrates, many of which are found in Australian tropical waters. Includes an interesting introduction to each phylum.

Australian Marine Life: The plants and animals of temperate waters (2nd edition). Graham J. Edgar. Reed Books (2008). This definitive (and large) guide to Australia's temperate marine life covers over 1,400 plants and animals, each with photo and brief notes on habitat, distribution and size.

GENERAL

Encyclopedia of Australian Wildlife (revised edition). Reader's Digest (2007). This comprehensive tome covers most major animal groups with interesting detail.

Reader's Digest Complete Book of Australian Birds (2nd edition). Reader's Digest (2007). This book goes beyond field guides, including excellent information about bird behaviour.

Reader's Digest Book of the Great Barrier Reef. Reader's Digest (1990). Although now out of print, this book provides an excellent overview of the reef and its creatures, with fine photographs.

Wild Habitats: A Natural History of Australian Ecosystems. Allan Fox and Steve Parish. ABC

Books (2007). Although a bit wordy at times, this book looks at Australia from the interesting perspective of habitats.

BACKGROUND READING
The Future Eaters. Tim Flannery. Reed New Holland (1998). One of Australia's most respected scientists airs some often controversial theories in this well-written, readable book about the impact humans have had on the Australasian ecosystem.
The Big Twitch. Sean Dooley. Allen and Unwin (2005). The author, a comedy writer, describes with humour his obsessive quest to see more than 700 Australian bird species in 12 months.

BOOKSHOP
Andrew Isles bookshop in Melbourne is Australia's leading natural history specialist bookshop. It can be found at the rear of 115–117 Greville Street, (PO Box 2305), Prahran 3181, Melbourne; tel: +61 (03) 9510 5750; fax: +61 (03) 9529 1256; www.andrewisles.com.

WEBSITES
The Australian Museum: **www.australianmuseum.net.au** (click on the 'Animals' link for a wealth of information).
State museums also often have good sites, for example the Queensland Museum: **www.qm.qld.gov.au**
ABC has a lively natural history site: **www.abc.net.au/science/scribblygum**

Birds Australia has upcoming events and a Bird finder section: **www.birdsaustralia.com.au**

Bird Observation and Conservation Australia: **www.boca.org.au** has an Events calendar on the 'Come birding' link. Non-members welcome.

For weather advice see: **www.bom.gov.au** and for road conditions: **www.racq.com.au/benefits_and_discounts/road_conditions**

For information on national parks check the appropriate state or territory site:
New South Wales: **www.environment.nsw.gov.au/nationalparks**
Northern Territory: **www.nt.gov.au/nreta/parks**
Queensland: **www.derm.qld.gov.au/parks_and_forests/index.html**
South Australia: **www.environment.sa.gov.au/parks**
Tasmania: **www.parks.tas.gov.au**
Victoria: **www.parkweb.vic.gov.au**
Western Australia: **www.dec.wa.gov.au/content/section/33/1558**